So You Want
to Be a
Social Worker

BOOKS IN THIS SERIES

So You Want to Be a Social Worker

(*Revised Edition*)

HELEN HARRIS PERLMAN

Harper & Row, Publishers
New York, Evanston, and London

1817

LIBRARY OF CONGRESS CATALOG CARD NUMBER: 77-106939

Contents

To tell you
about this book—

Eight years ago the first edition of this book was written. That's a long time ago in your lifetime if you're a high school or even a college student. It's a very short time in the life of a profession. Yet many things are changing swiftly and social work as a profession and as a career is one of them. So it became imperative to revise this book, really to rewrite it almost completely if it is to give you an accurate picture of what social work is today and your possible place in it.

Within this past decade "the invisible poor" have become not only sharply visible but highly audible too. Racial and civil rights problems, the miseries of ghetto living, bad housing, insufficient medical care, delinquency, violence, the apparently spreading sense of alienation among many people, the desperate search for identity and purpose among the young—these and other symptoms of social sickness and malaise are suddenly open for everyone who has eyes to see and ears to hear. The eyes and ears of social workers have long been trained on personal and social ills. Indeed the social worker is usually right in the center of "where the action is." So changes in social work as a profession and social work as a career are responsive to changing times and a shifting center of concern.

One of the changes that has occurred since the first edition of this book is that social welfare has become everyone's business. That's a slight exaggeration, of course, but the fact is that there has probably been no time in history when so many people have been so keenly concerned with the plight of the poor, or with the problems of achieving personal and interpersonal "happiness" that are to be found in every socioeconomic class. Our government's commitment to "war on poverty," to ensuring and implementing all people's rights to open opportunities, has resulted in numerous and widespread programs and projects to provide such opportunities and, more, to involve the maximum feasible participation of the persons who are to be their beneficiaries. To these ends a considerable sector of social workers—and of education for social work—is concentrating on so-called "community work." This involves the organization of indigenous and neighborhood groups, developing workable projects, finding supporting funds, assessing, consulting, offering direction, negotiating, coordinating, and so on. As you will see in the chapter on where social workers work, this movement of social work toward the mobilization of the heretofore untapped powers for social change is growing in impetus and strength. More community organizers and community workers are needed and wanted today than ever before.

Along with this there has come a revived interest among caseworkers and group workers in meeting the many problems, beyond those of economic need, of the long and chronically poor. Reaching the "hard-to-reach" has become a compelling interest among those social workers who deal with the social and personal disorganization and malfunctioning of individuals and families. The hard-to-reach are, typically, people who have felt so outcast from society's mainstreams, so cut off or discriminated against, so hopeless and hostile that they have turned their faces away from the kinds of help that are there to be had if they would reach for them. So helping people to want help—to trust a doctor, to talk to their child's teacher, to believe that neighborhood house clubs might be pleasurable for their child, to ask a caseworker what to do about their fourteen-year-old pregnant daughter—such "reaching out" is a growing effort in social agencies.

One fact that became very clear as social work widened its horizons and perspectives is that there simply could not be produced enough social workers with full professional education and training to meet the vast spectrum of human need that was being uncovered. Therefore social work has faced up to the plain necessity to draw upon new manpower resources. In the past few years social agencies, social work's professional organization and its professional schools have agreed on the need to develop and use a vast corps of "paraprofessionals" (those who are "kin" to professionals, who work side by side with them), of "social work aides" and /or "social work technicians." Of course people with a bachelor's degree or lesser education have been working as social workers for many years, most of them as "relief investigators" in the public assistance agencies, but in many other places too.

The shift that has occurred in professional social work's view of the "nonprofessional" is twofold: (1) he is seen as necessary, essential, if there is to be minimal coverage of human beings' social needs; (2) he can be prepared to deal with many aspects of the social welfare job not only by on-the-job training (which has long been the case) but by the inclusion of certain basic social welfare and social work courses in college and even in junior colleges. Thus today there have sprung up hundreds of courses in undergraduate education to provide some groundwork for entering a career as a social work aide or paraprofessional. Chapter Five tells you about this.

Many other new developments have occurred in the less than ten years since the first edition of this book was published. Salary scales for professional social workers have risen remarkably. Black, Spanish-speaking, American Indian student-applicants to schools of social work are being searched for, recruited, and offered excellent scholarships—but you will read of all this for yourself.

I have tried to focus on what I think you want to know, you who are turning over in your mind whether or not you want to become a social worker. You will find the who, what, how, where, and why of social work and social workers set out for you here. I hope it will make you want to be one!

Helen Harris Perlman

University of Chicago
July, 1969

one: *Who and what are social workers?*

The minute you think about entering some profession or career line you think "What will it be like, for *me?*" and "Who are the people that are the profession's (or occupation's) workers? What do they actually *do?*" It's all very well for someone to give you a definition and a description of any kind of work; but under the words you're reading or hearing you're wondering, "What are the kinds of things I'd be doing every working day? What would I have to act like? What would I have to become?"

So, instead of starting with an explanation, I'll introduce you to some typical young social workers—the kind of people who would be your colleagues or "work-mates" if you were to be a social worker. If you make yourself invisible you can watch them in action. Meet five of them—

Mary Wright and Don Hart, both caseworkers; Judy Foster and Gabe Healy and Tom Goodwin, group workers and community workers.

We'll take casework first because, currently at least, about 70 percent of social workers are caseworkers, which is to say that they focus their professional attention and help on individuals and/or families who are experiencing trouble in some tasks or relationships in their everyday lives.

Don Hart is a caseworker in a family and child welfare agency, an agency that has a long tradition of help to people with problems in marriage, in their work or school adjustments, in parent-child relationships. Counseling and guidance and therapeutic problem-solving is Don's "thing."

Mary Wright is a caseworker too in a newly set up child health clinic in the ghetto, the Parkside Clinic (no park has been in sight for years!). Her wish is to do everything she can to better the lives of ghetto kids. And "everything she can" needs doing too! She counsels and guides at times as Don does, but she does a lot of other things too, as you'll see when you come along with her. (We'll visit her first—because the waiting room of Parkside Clinic is already, early in the morning, filled up with mothers and children.)

Mary Wright has her master's degree from a school of social work. Immediately after her graduation she married John Wright, the young man she'd been "going steady" with for several years. He continued with his law school studies and she took a job right away in order, as she and her husband said, to work his way through school. Her first job was as caseworker in a public child welfare agency. She learned a lot there about babies and youngsters whose parents were unable to love them or to give them adequate care, and about what placement of children in foster homes or institutions does to children's minds and hearts—sometimes hurting them, sometimes healing them.

The medical staff of doctors and nurses who undertook to man the city's new Parkside Clinic for Children were glad to get Mary Wright as one of their social workers, partly because she brought so much knowledge and understanding of children and parents and their needs and the ways to help them, partly because of the person she is.

Mary is black and Parkside is largely a black ghetto. (Just the same some of Mary's first clients were light-skinned Puerto Ricans, and Mary had to get and use a Spanish-speaking casework aide as her interpreter.) Mary, as you will see, is open, friendly, strong, dedicated to helping the disadvantaged person, no matter what his color. Her dedication is "informed" by her knowledge and know-how, so while her feelings move her they do not run away with her. One of these days Mary and John plan to start a family of their own. But in the meantime Mary Wright is deeply involved in "her families," the black and brown and white mothers and children whose health problems bring them for medical care but who also need many kinds of social care and help.

On this morning when you are to observe her, her first client is already waiting to see her when at nine o'clock she walks into the cool, clean clinic from the dusty, trash-blown pavement outside. She is anxious-looking Mrs. Brown with her six-year-old Frankie. Mrs. Brown greets Mary Wright tensely. Frankie is to see the doctor for his weekly checkup this morning, and at the same time his mother will see the social worker to talk over what she can do about this sick and troubling child of hers.

Frankie was brought to the clinic several weeks ago with symptoms that the doctors recognized at once as those of lead poisoning. Lead poisoning is not uncommon in Parkside.

It is found in children who pick at broken places in their house walls and eat the crumbling chunks of painted plaster. It is thought that some dietary deficiency or some body chemistry need creates this unlikely appetite. For individual children brought to a doctor there is treatment to be had that will prevent blood poisoning, neurological damage, and even death. But in tenement houses old paint is full of lead and tens of children may eat at it, unnoticed by their parents. So the problem is a bigger one than Frankie Brown—this Mary Wright, social worker, knows. And one of the things she must do today is check with her fellow social worker Gabe Healy in the Neighborhood Community House about the next meeting of the Tenants' Organization. Gabe and she have helped some of their clients who've complained of inadequate heating, broken stairs, nonflushing toilets to form a group to take joint action about violations of rental contracts or housing codes. Perhaps Mr. and Mrs. Brown would like to join them to report and hasten repairs on their broken and peeling walls.

Back to Mrs. Brown. She leaves Frankie in the waiting room with a picture book, admonishing him to be good and be quiet while she talks to Mrs. Wright. Frankie looks stonily at his picture book. Mrs. Brown follows Mary Wright into her small but cheerful office, anxious, tight, pent-up.

Frankie is just unmanageable, she begins. He is either so drowsy and lazy that he seems sick or else so restless that he drives her and her husband crazy. He squirms, wiggles, runs wild, spills his milk, tries to break places in the hallway walls to find plaster. He won't go to sleep because he is afraid he will die. She has warned him of this fate many times—and now she sees that he believes it. But what can she do? She slaps and spanks him, tells him to be good and he won't die;

only bad children are punished. Her husband is no help—he says she's to blame for Frankie's trouble—after all she's with him all day. . . .

Mary Wright listens attentively, sympathetically. If her hackles rise when she hears that a child is slapped for being afraid she controls her natural reaction because she knows that Mrs. Brown, like any of us, could not take help from someone who censured her. She also knows that parents are sometimes cruel to their children simply out of their own combined ignorance and desperation. So she hears Mrs. Brown out and notices the little beads of sweat that gather on Mrs. Brown's dark wrinkled forehead as she quietly but tensely tells her story.

Mrs. Brown has told Mary that she herself was raised by a strict grandmother who drove into her head that she must better herself. She was glad to have married a good conscientious man like her husband who worked hard and long hours (though, unskilled as he was, he could earn only minimum wages) and they wanted their only child to "make it out of this ghetto." And now Frankie is only six years old and they can't even control him. His first-grade teacher, she goes on to say breathlessly, tells her he's not learning anything. He is restless, pays no attention . . .

Mary Wright asks clarifying questions now and then, indicating by her words and facial responses that she feels for Mrs. Brown in her desperation. She knows that without help now Frankie may get physically better but psychologically worse. She makes a mental note (along with that about the Tenants' Organization) to ask the doctor whether Frankie's restlessness has a physical-neurological basis. But even if it does, there is this mother to be helped to tolerate what she finds intolerable and to understand that her child is anxious

and afraid, not just "mean." And there is Frankie's father,
who is shrugging off his place and responsibility in his son's
life and leaving his already troubled wife to bear both guilt
and blame.

Mary begins to test out Mrs. Brown's capacity to understand Frankie. Why does she think Frankie is afraid to die?
Does he believe he's bad? What gives him this feeling? Are
there any ways Mrs. Brown can think of by which she, his
mother, his main source of love, can give him the feeling that
he's good, worth her love, that he is someone she is pleased
with?

So the laborious work of casework "treatment" begins. It
would be easy, of course, to tell Mrs. Brown, kindly, what she
was doing wrong and why, and to explain what she ought to
do and why. But one of the facts of life that professional
caseworkers know in depth is that people do not just take
other people's judgments and advice or, if they do, they often
use them badly. People, rather, must be helped, step by step,
to find their own explanations and solutions. Such guidance
by the caseworker gives a person a sense of his own capacity
and power, and his solutions, when self-powered, are more
likely to work out.

Casework counseling of the mother is not all. Mary raises
the question of Mr. Brown's becoming a partner in helping
Frankie get over his present behavior and fear. He won't, says
Mrs. Brown. Mary Wright asks if she might try to draw him
in. He works every day, Mrs. Brown objects. Mary reminds
her that the clinic is open one night a week and she'd be glad
to see them then. "See us together?" asks Mrs. Brown, half-
relieved. Mary Wright affirms this good idea: "You made
Frankie together; so you can be parents helping Frankie together." It's agreed.

There's another resource that Mary Wright may tap and use later. It's a small, informal parents' group that meets in the clinic one evening a week over coffee and cookies. They talk about kids and parents, how hard it is to raise kids these days. Sometimes one of the doctors meets with them and tells about some common problems of health or sickness; sometimes a nutritionist nurse talks with them about children's food fads and diet; sometimes one of the social workers. Mary Wright, one of them, talks with the parents on the child-rearing problems they have. Sometimes the parents teach one another. It's a kind of social education group, fun for those parents (mostly mothers) who have so little chance to get out for a bit of time to themselves, and often comforting, too, to find that their problems are shared by other people. But Mary Wright is not yet suggesting this group for the Browns. This may come later, after the nature of their problems with Frankie and themselves is clarified and they have had the individualized kind of counseling they need.

It's agreed then: Mrs. Brown will ask her husband to come to the clinic with her next Thursday night—and Mary Wright will send him a note inviting him also. Frankie may come along with them because there is a social work aide who takes care of and plays with the children on the clinic's open evening when parents who cannot come daytimes are seen.

Part of the job ahead, Mary sees, is to help these driving, anxious young parents take their eyes off their upward goals for a bit and turn them to their unwell, love-hungry, and frightened little boy. Another part is to get the family's living conditions bettered. With a housing shortage and their inability to pay high rents the probability is that they must remain in their present apartment. But, under the guidance of Gabe Healy, the community worker for Parkside Neighborhood House, there's the Tenants' Organization being formed to bring pressure against landlords who violate housing ordinances.

There's another vital area in Frankie's life that needs attention too. It's school. Here he already spends five hours of every day. Unless he finds those five hours interesting or pleasurable, unless his teacher gives him the warmth and acceptance he needs, school will become something to be feared and resisted. This very afternoon, Mary Wright decides (having checked out with Mrs. Brown that it would be okay) she will stop at the Lincoln School and make an appointment to talk to Frankie's teacher and explain something of what he's suffering.

Mary Wright jots down these "to-dos"—one case has so many angles!—the Browns, the school, the landlord and/or the Tenants' Organization, the doctor, maybe the parents' group later on. Then she pulls herself together to leave the clinic and go out to her next family, that of Mrs. Lopez.

Mrs. Brown wants help, desperately. Mrs. Lopez does not. Mrs. Lopez says, by her actions if not by her words, "Just leave me and my sick kids alone. I don't trust anybody to help me."

Briefly about the Lopez family: Mr. Lopez died four years ago, shortly after the family had moved into Parkside on their arrival from Puerto Rico. Mrs. Lopez was left with three children, pregnant with a fourth. She and her husband had come to the United States full of hope of starting a new life and she found herself in a cold, harsh slum, in a dark and dirty flat, widowed, forced to apply for and live on relief, unable to speak the language of the people around her, unable to feel connected with her neighbors. The color of her and her children's skin was not too different from the skin of the American "blacks" who populated the neighborhood, but their backgrounds were very different. "I am Spanish," she would say, over and over, as if to explain all her troubles. She could not (or refused to?) speak any English. She would not talk to her relief investigator about anything except (through an interpreter) the needs that she and her children had that the relief budget did not meet. The nurse in the school the children attend (Pedro, 10, Francisco, 8, and Milagros, 6; Dolores, 3, is still at home) had reported that they all seemed under- or malnourished, that they had frequent sore throats and colds that kept them out of school, that Milagros frequently complained of headaches. When the relief caseworker had tried to get Mrs. Lopez to take the children to the Parkside Clinic she had met with Mrs. Lopez's usual "Leave me alone. Nobody cares for me. I will care for my children." So she had called Mary Wright to ask if Parkside Clinic would "reach out" to Mrs. Lopez.

This is what Mary Wright was starting off to do this morning. She had arranged to take with her one of the clinic's social work aides, José Chavez, a Puerto Rican young man who, after taking some social welfare courses in the city junior college, had been hired by the Parkside Clinic as an interpreter. But he turns out to be more than this. His natural sunny warmth and unobtrusive sensitivity to others makes him a carrier of good feelings, not just a walking vocabulary.

"The problem is," Mary Wright explains to José as they walk through the littered, children-jumping streets to Mrs. Lopez's flat, "that a person like Mrs. Lopez must be afraid to reach out for anyone's help. She probably feels she's been betrayed and hurt by everyone: her husband didn't choose to die, of course, but just the same he left her penniless, burdened, in a strange place. The Aid to Dependent Children's relief grants *are* very hard to manage on, and they force her to live in a house and area she hates. She has no social relationships, no chance for getting out from four dirty walls and four growing children. And now along comes the school and says, 'We're concerned about your kids. ...' But Mrs. Lopez must be feeling 'What about *me!* Why doesn't someone care for *me*, for *my* hurts and headaches and health!' "

José sees this. So they plan together about how this first interview (if Mrs. Lopez will let them in the door) will focus on how Mrs. Lopez sees and feels her troubles—not on what the outside world reports—and then they will try to hook the clinic and its medical and social services into what she wants. Some of the things Mary Wright speaks of as they walk along are that José will offer to call for Mrs. Lopez and bring her and the children to the clinic, just for a look-see; that there are some Spanish-speaking clubs or groups for adults in the Neighborhood House that Mrs. Lopez might want to connect with; that the clinic doctor who sees the children must be alerted to giving Mrs. Lopez all the credit that's due her for her care of her children before she can be expected to work with changes of diet or whatever it is that keeps them below par. Probably, after medical examinations, extra money for special diets could be got from ADC to be included in the relief grant. But first to give Mrs. Lopez the proof that *her* welfare was of concern to the community. (There is no space to tell you what happened in the interview except one small incident that has significance: at its end Mrs. Lopez turned to Mary Wright and said, "Thank you" and "Good-by" in English!)

Back at the clinic there are all the behind-the-scenes jobs to be done. Confer with Frankie's doctor so each knows what the other is doing and why. Call Gabe Healy and tell him the landlord of the Browns' building has obviously done nothing about the repairs he was to make. Will he take this to the Tenants' Organization he's developing—or should it be reported higher up, to the city housing authorities? Should Mary, together with Mr. and Mrs. Brown (if they want this), appear at the next meeting of the Tenants' Organization and tell about the Browns' experiences with this landlord? Report to the Lincoln School nurse on the first moves made toward Mrs. Lopez. Oh, yes, and call Don Hart about the meeting they're planning for the casework section of the chapter of their professional association (National Association of Social Workers). It's to discuss methods of "Helping Resistant Clients."

"Resistant clients" occur not only in the ghetto. They happen in any level of society, as Don Hart well knows. When Mary Wright's call comes Don's secretary says he'll call her back. He's deep in an interview with a highly articulate, educated, successful businessman who cannot (will not?) see why his wife feels they need to do something about their marriage situation. If she wants to talk to "some shrink"—a caseworker or a psychiatrist—he will be perfectly glad to give her the money for it. But as far as he's concerned he is content to let things be. The children?—Oh, he doubts very much that his car-crazy, girl-crazy, hop-headed fifteen-year-old son or his little three-year-old daughter pays any attention to what's going on between him and his wife. Unless, of course, she talks to them about her really crazy imaginings.

The family agency where Don Hart works is concerned with the growth and maintenance of good sound family life at every level of society. Middle-class people can bleed and suffer too when treasured relationships turn sour or are torn

apart. Their children can become delinquent or personally
unhappy to the point of inability to study or sleep or make
friends. So Don Hart's agency offers guidance and therapeutic help to families or individuals at any level of the social and
economic scale. Those able to pay a fee for counseling do so;
those who cannot need not. Beyond the difference that
money makes—and it makes a great difference in people's
lives, no doubt about it, both in buying the necessities of
decent living and in providing some of the small luxuries that
cushion our lives—there are some common human problems
and wants that are not classifiable by economic class or color.
So people of many kinds come to Don Hart's agency, asking
for help to become better parents or to cope with interfamily
conflicts or sometimes privately personal ones.

There was Mrs. Black, for instance, who had first come to
ask that they guide her to some "good" home for the aged
where she could place her old father. He had lived in her
home since her mother died and her husband and children
had "loved grandpa." But now he was growing senile; he
would wander away unless he was watched every minute, he
was sometimes irrational, and so on. When Don was able to
locate a high-standard home for the aged (and the Blacks
could afford to pay its costs) Mrs. Black suddenly found herself immobilized. "I can't," she said. "I can't put my father
out." Yet there was the fact that he was making life for the
family one of continuous tension and that he himself needed
custodial care. But Mrs. Black wept and vacillated, torn by
guilt and caught between her father and her young family. It
took her several interviews with Don Hart to talk through
and think through and feel through her conflicts and indeci-
sions, and the reasons for them, and the consequences of
placing her father versus keeping him at home, and the "bad

child" feelings that had risen in her, feelings she thought had died and been buried when she left childhood. With Don's help she was able to come through what was for her an emotional crisis that might otherwise have ended in retreat and bitterness.

Now, as you're watching Don, he is making a strong and firm statement to Mr. White, the impatient husband of the woman who wants help with their marriage. "I can tell you that your wife is very disturbed," he says quietly, firmly. "I can also tell you, out of our long experience with families, that little pitchers have big ears and that children are not only aware of but deeply affected by even covered-up hostilities between their parents. Maybe 'car-crazy, girl-crazy' is what you want your son to be." Mr. White shakes his head angrily. "I suggest that you can't lose anything but an hour or two of your time by consenting to come in here with your wife to talk some things over with me. And you might even gain something—something even *you* might want." Mr. White grins. "You're a good salesman," he says to Don. "Want a job?" "I've got a job," says Don, "you and your family." They make an appointment and shake hands on it. Maybe Mr. White will cancel it. But maybe he'll find it less necessary to keep blinders over his eyes once discussions open between him and his wife, managed and guided by the neutral but concerned helper Don Hart.

Don's next appointment is waiting. It's Josie Green— fifteen, high school sophomore, large gold earrings dangling below her newly napped African hairdo, perfect featured. She'd be a beautiful young adolescent except for being too fat. She's been "a compulsive eater" this past year (since her father left), she reported when she was first seen by Don, "and nobody can make me stop. I like it!" But she has stopped, within the past three weeks, and she reports the minute she comes into Don's office and plumps herself into the chair, "Another three pounds off this week!" "Is that what your new hairdo celebrates?" Don asks. "Yup," says Josie smugly. "Like it?"

Three months ago the high school counselor in Josie's school had called Don and asked if he would talk to Josie. Some dramatic change had come over her, her teachers reported. Bright, perky, this youngster with a high IQ and a most promising school record had slumped in her work and in her interest. She'd looked sullen (or was it sad?). She often cut classes or was absent for alleged illness, was often impertinent to her teachers, had begun to put on excess weight. The counselor's effort to draw her out brought only shrugs and "nothing's wrong" from Josie.

Social caseworkers have no magic ways by which to get to people in trouble. But, based on a lot of experience with such people, they often are good guessers about what might be wrong. Besides, the fact that they are "outsiders" to the situation that's making the trouble makes them seem less prejudiced—and be so. In Josie's case it helped, too, that the social worker was a man, because her rage was at her mother and "all women" who "run men down."

Josie's deepest love, Don learned in talking with her, was for her father. He had been "kicked out of the house" by her mother because of his chronic drinking and failure to hold steady work. Josie's mother told Don *her* side of the story— how she had always worked hard as a domestic, how she wanted "the best" for her children, how much hope she had put in Josie's capability and success. But Josie was always "for her father," feeling sorry for him, telling her mother he was "sick, not bad." When he did not return after Mrs. Green had

"kicked him out" Josie "began to pine." Then she grew silent
and sullen and sloppy and began to miss school and ate, ate,
ate all day long—she'd "eat two giant chocolate bars at one
sitting," said her mother incredulously.

Josie has had a lot to talk over with Don Hart in her weekly
interviews. She has found that he deeply understands her
aching compassion "for all underdogs." She saw her father as
one of these. Attached to this feeling was her growing sense
that "all blacks are underdogs," and from this a sense that she
was an underdog too. She has found Don something like a
father—even though he is pale-white and straight-sandy-
haired and probably only old enough to be a brother—but
he's been a "father" in that he has attended to *her,* to what's
good for her, to what she feels and wants, and from under his
gentle attentiveness there emerges his firm sense of strength
and direction that makes her feel safe. He got the teachers
"off her back"—those who, out of their concern for her, it's
true, kept telling her to diet, to study—and he convinced
them she would do so "when she's ready." And he was right.
When he had restored her sense of selfness, when he had
helped her see her separateness as a unique human being
from both her father and her mother, to express and feel her
own inner strengths and drives—she was ready to use her
fine head and will power again.

Today Don suggests she might begin to think about
whether she wants and needs to come to see him every week.
He won't leave *her*—this he assures her; but *she* may want to
think about leaving *him* in a couple of months. Josie's brows
grow dark; then she says, "I'll think it over. I'll decide with
that brain you say I have." Don smiles broadly and supports
her "self-determination."

By the way, I put you into Don's office without an adequate

introduction. Like Mary Wright, Don Hart is a professional social worker with a graduate degree. You'd never notice him in a roomful of people—this slight, bespectacled young man —but once you'd talked with him you'd be drawn to him. For one thing he's got a quick and ready humor (and a good wide smile); for another he's got a way of cocking his head and listening to you, carefully, as if he really was interested in what you said, even about the weather. He's been out of school four years, is specializing in helping people with their personal and interpersonal conflicts. To that end he's taking some postgraduate courses in personality problems and their treatment.

But he remains a social worker, which is to say he never loses sight of the social factors in people's lives that shape and color their feelings and their objective realities. He keeps one foot in other forms of social service too. For instance, for some months he's been meeting with a group of teachers at one of the city's junior high schools as leader of their discussions of adolescents, their particular psychological needs and problems and ways of helping them. (Incidentally, that's how Josie was referred to him—by one of the teachers in that group.) Another group Don meets with regularly is a "family life education" group of youngish parents who are interested in anticipating the normal kinds of problems that are expectable in the life of any family and in preparing for coping with them or even preventing their happening. Don is an active member of the Social Action Committee of his city's chapter of the National Association of Social Workers. (So is Mary Wright, as you'd expect.) Along with all this—sometime, somehow, Don studies, he dates Judy Foster (a group worker whom you'll meet shortly), and he "keeps fit" by playing a mean game of tennis and squash—and occasionally picking on his old guitar.

Judy Foster—"Now *there's* a gal," Don Hart would say. You may share his admiration as you watch her now with the Soul Queens, a group of noisy, laughing, pushing adolescent girls coming into the room in the Neighborhood House. You'll see Judy in the midst of them, shining brown eyes, slick short-cut hair capping her well-shaped head. She's the littlest one among them, all but drowned out by their size and noise. For a while it was nip and tuck as to whether Judy was going to be able to make it with the Soul Queens. For one thing, several of them did not want a white social worker—and they said so, loud and clear. But, as several others pointed out, there was no one else available on the staff at the time they decided they wanted an adult leader. There *was* Gabe Healy, also a graduate group worker, like Judy, but several of the Queens felt as strongly against a *man* as others felt against a *white*. Judy had courageously and frankly faced it out with them and suggested they "give it a try." So they did. Now most of the Queens don't know, or care, what color Judy is.

For one thing Judy knows an awful lot about the kinds of things that bug you when you're twelve to fourteen years old. Another thing, she doesn't shout or shut you up when you want to talk about fooling around with boys and that stuff, but she says let's talk about it, straight out. Sometimes she's strict, no fooling, but not mean. Like when one of the kids got herself in trouble and began to show and she couldn't admit it or go to a doctor. Judy Foster took her into her office and laid down the law about what might happen to her and her baby if she didn't go to the doctor and tell her mother and all that, and afterwards, when her mother nearly killed her, Judy found a place where she could stay and be taken care of till the baby came. The Soul Queens had a lot of talking to do with Judy about all that, you can be sure.

This afternoon, though, they're planning a party. They want to invite the Blue Bloods, a group of somewhat older boys whom Gabe Healy lured into the House from the street corner when they had been a gang involved in petty delinquency. Maybe they still are—Gabe isn't sure at all—but he's trying to involve them not only in using the athletic equipment in the House but in thinking up and carrying out small projects that will benefit the neighborhood. And thus bring them the rewards of recognition and praise. They've just finished organizing and supervising an all-kid cleanup campaign in a five-block area; the neighborhood newspaper printed a blurry picture of them with their names underneath. They liked that. Among them are a couple of boys who, Gabe thinks, have tremendous potential for leadership. If he can get even only these two youngsters on to interests and opportunities that will mean "upward bound" for them Gabe feels the total effort with the Blue Bloods will have been worthwhile.

Naturally, when the Soul Queens think about inviting the Blue Bloods to a party they are doubled up with laughing and screaming about who's going to go for whom. Judy kids along with them but after a while she calls the Queen Bee's attention to the fact that they're getting nowhere fast. How do you have a party? How do you "invite"? What will you eat and drink? What will make it fun and not just a brawl? So they reluctantly settle down to the work of planning, choosing, deciding. Judy intervenes at times, pointing out that some people haven't been given a chance to express themselves, or suggesting that how something is likely to turn out is a better way of thinking about it than just whether it's "fun" or not.

In short, the whole purpose behind Judy Foster's leadership is not that the Soul Queens or any other group she's interested in should simply have a good time, but rather that they should repeatedly experience that there are better rather than worse ways of managing the conduct of their large and small affairs and, further, that they should know that there are adults who care about them, respect them, and yet have some guidance to give that is useful to them.

Matter of fact, these were among the reasons why Judy chose to make group work the social work method of her concentration: that she might be able to influence people, young or old, to see and feel themselves as members of social groups and be aware always of the effect of their attitudes and actions on others as well as the other way round. Nevertheless, she and Don Hart find many things in common between casework and group work, and when, on their dates, they slip into "shop talk" they get and give many useful pointers to each other, Don as the expert on individual psychology and behavior, Judy as the expert on groups. In his casework Don often deals with groups—as when he sees family members together or when he has his "family life education" sessions. Judy in her group work often deals with individuals—as when she must pull out one of the group members to talk to her separately or when she must talk to a parent in order to give better help to some child or to the parent herself (or himself).

In fact that's what Judy is about to do when the Soul Queens tumble themselves out of the Neighborhood House, laughing and shoving and chattering. First she must call back Mary Wright to say yes, there is a group of Spanish-speaking mothers who come to the Neighborhood House regularly to "socialize," to feel "at home" with one another, speaking their mother tongue. At the same time they get some help in the new situations they encounter and the new ways they must learn if they and their children are to make a go of it. Yes, there would be room for Mrs. Lopez. She (Judy) will meet her before the group begins if she can be brought in early and will try to make her feel at home. Judy, incidentally, speaks Spanish. It was the language she took in high school and for two years of college and while her vocabulary and accent are "infantile" (Judy's own assessment) she is able to communicate. Often her clients are glad to find her as helpless with their beautiful language as they are with hers. They can laugh together at their mistakes on both sides.

Now Judy is off to call on the mother of one of the little boys who comes to an after-school tutoring program. It's a program Judy and the social work aides worked out with the neighborhood school. For kids who are already having trouble with their reading and writing and numbers in the first three grades (usually little boys) the three "aides" give tutoring. In order to make learning different from what blocks them in school they teach and learn by games and by small "fun" projects. Now they are planning a show and they have laboriously printed and crayoned invitations to their parents to come see it.

But Clayton's mother won't come. Clayton's pale-blue eyes were brimming with tears when he told this to his reading helper. Judy can guess why. Clayton's family have recently come up from Tennessee. They have found themselves in a ghetto of mixed color and in an urban culture that is totally foreign, even hostile, to them. Clayton's mother wants none of it, Judy can imagine. So Judy has asked Clayton to tell his mother she'd like to come by to see her—and this afternoon she will knock at the door and, if she can get a foot in, will begin the work of helping someone know that even in the big

impersonal city there are pockets of concern and understanding—and opportunity too.

We mentioned Gabe before in connection with the Blue
Bloods. You wouldn't think to look at him that he was married
and the father of a pair of four-year-old twin boys. ("Big
league ballplayers," says Gabe. "Harvard professors," says his
wife.) Dribbling the ball on the basketball court or sprawled
in a chair in a bull session, Gabe would be taken for one of
the older adolescent boys he works with except that he's
more powerfully built, more securely knit together. You can
see how adolescents would be drawn to him—he seems
easygoing, open, relaxed. But at the same time he knows who
he is and what he's there for and where he wants to go—and
this gives the fellows who cluster around him a sense that he's
a kind of anchor person when they're likely to be full of
unease about themselves, full of conflicts and identity questions.

In addition to the Blue Bloods Gabe is working in a special
project that's been set up under government funds to try to
"rehabilitate" groups of "unemployable" young men. This
means to try to get these men, first of all, to *want* to work
(many were early school dropouts, some became drug users,
others lived off of their wives' working or by illegal means),
to get them to want to take the necessary pains and training
that regular work involves, and then to find or make the job
openings. All this takes group work and a lot of community
work too, because it's not just the "unemployables" whose
attitudes must undergo change. There is also a big job to be
done in persuading the people who are prospective employers of the need and rightness of their cooperation. So this
means evenings when Gabe and his fellow workers get themselves invited to meet with and speak to organizations of

small businessmen, church groups, and men's social clubs, to interpret, persuade, exhort—do whatever needs to be done to get the employing community's interest and trust in the project.

Gabe is a kind of caseworker too. At times, like Judy, he must give some special and sustained attention to one or another of the men he's working with to try to rev up his lagging interest or motivation or to find out what seems to be blocking him.

Gabe "digs" this Parkside area, the needs of the people in it, and the help that social work can give. As he'll tell you easily and with the quiet sincerity that is his, he himself was a kid in this community and was "partly brought up" in this Neighborhood House. A fatherless boy whose mother worked long hours, he came to the House almost every day after school, to "belong" to its clubs or to read in its small branch library. In those days its personnel was all white—but Gabe found no reason not to trust them and found many resources in the House by which to feed his social and intellectual hungers. As an adolescent he began to be given part-time jobs with groups of younger kids, and it was through the efforts of the head resident that he went off to four years of college, partly on an athletic scholarship. He married his long-time girlfriend when he was graduated and took civil service examinations and scored high enough to get a supervisory job in the post office. But he hated the monotony of paper work and, although he and his wife lived a long way off from Parkside (in a newly built bungalow in a newly developed neighborhood), he started dropping in to volunteer whatever of his services they could use.

Suddenly he became aware of how much this community needed his help. The neighborhood he had known had

grown far more crowded, was rapidly deteriorating, sub-
jected to streams of heavy traffic, to building rot, to proliferat-
ing taverns and bookie joints. "I'd really like to put myself
whole into that place," he had said to his wife one night.
Then one of the social workers at the House told him about
the tuition and maintenance scholarships that college graduates could get in schools of social work. Next year Gabe and
his wife were off across the country to the school of his
choice. Two years later Gabe was back at the House—"This
is kinda my home base," he said—but now Gabriel Healy was
a "senior group worker." Before too long he will probably be
made the director of the House and its whole program of
group and community work.

Gabe excuses himself. He's got to get out of his sweat shirt
and into a jacket and tie. He has an appointment uptown with
a staff member of the city's Community Welfare Council. If
you'll come along with him you'll meet another community
worker (the last of the social workers I'll introduce you to
today). He's Tom Goodwin, who is one of the community
planning and research staff of the coordinating council of all
the city's social agencies.

Like the others you've met, Tom is a professionally trained
social worker. He spent three years after graduation as a
caseworker and then as supervisor for a huge public child
welfare program. He wanted, he said, to have the direct
experience, not just the head knowledge, of the problems of
neglected and dependent and abused children, and of their
helpless parents, and then to know firsthand what programs
and helping means actually served them and what did not.
For the past three years he has been on the staff of the
Community Welfare Council. Among other jobs he heads its
child welfare section. What this means is that in regular

stocktaking with the executives of the various child welfare
agencies in the community (heads of children's adoption and
foster care programs, of children's treatment institutions,
children's day care and nursery facilities—and so on) he
keeps informed on what policies and programs for child care
are, what they're accomplishing or failing to accomplish and
why, what new or unmet needs there are that require planning for and building and putting into action.

Tom and Gabe have been good friends over the past year,
since they've come to know one another. They often disagree
about how to go about doing things—but they're strong allies
on the ends they're after. Tom is president of the local National Association of Social Workers chapter and Gabe is
president-elect, taking Tom's place next year, so they've had
a lot of professional interest and business together. Tom entered social work as an idealist. His parents were strongly
against his vocational choice. His father, a prosperous building contractor, expected his only son to follow in his foot-
steps, and he was appalled the day Tom came home and told
him he had decided he wanted to do "another kind of building—*people* building." "You're just some kind of starry-eyed
idealist," said his father. Tom's professional training disciplined him not to give up his ideals but to pay close attention
to the facts and data that had to be considered along the way
to achieving goals. Gabe, on the other hand, started with the
nitty-gritty of everyday practical life problems that he knew
in every detail, and he, in turn, has learned to lift up his eyes
from what *is* to take a good look at what *ought* to be and how
it can be made to happen. So these two social workers, Tom
and Gabe, are bound together by their common goals and
each enjoys the other for his difference of background, and
they respect and often enjoy their differences of approach.

(Incidentally, Tom's father has swallowed his disappoint-
ment and listens with growing interest to Tom's accounts of
work-in-progress. He has doubled his contribution to the
Community Chest Drive "because I believe in it," he says.)

Gabe Healy has come to consult with Tom on a plan that
he and the Neighborhood House director, together with
some of the leaders of the newly sprouting Neighborhood
Organization of Women (NOW), have been talking about.

The plan Gabe brings to Tom at the Council is for the
development of a day care center for Parkside. It could be
started in the Neighborhood House but as Gabe and the
director and the planning committee of NOW have visual-
ized it it will need much more space to accommodate a hundred or more children. And it will need all the furnishings—
cots, little chairs and tables, play contraptions and toys, a
kitchen and all its equipment, laundry and tot toilets. And
then, when all the building and physical equipment have
been planned and purchased (and where to find all the
money it will cost?) there will need to be found (and trained
and paid) all the people without whom a day care center is
just rooms with things in them. The people (as both Gabe and
Tom know well) must be a core staff with professional knowledge about little children: nurses, a visiting doctor, nursery
school teachers, a social worker in residence or available for
frequent consultation, a cook. With the core staff at the center
there will be need for many paid aides and volunteers—to
play with the children, to help feed them, comfort them,
cuddle them—to do all the mothering, caring, teaching—
things that little ones need for their good physical and psychological growth.

Tom Goodwin nods with interest and pleasure as Gabe lays
out his plans. He puts in an idea here and there. Gabe likes

it or argues it; Tom argues back. In a way they're like two
boys planning an adventure—imaginative, buoyed up by a
happy prospect. But alternately they're in their practical social worker skins again, considering where to find money,
how to get support for the project, what personnel problems
and possibilities there will be, and so on.

The need for such a day care facility in Parkside is elo-
quently put forward by Gabe. He knows the mothers of Parkside and the needs of their babies too. Some of the mothers
work, and leave their preschool children in the care of neighbors or women who take children in by the day and give
them little more than their meals. Some mothers would like
to work, but not at the risk of inadequate care for their little
ones. Some mothers who don't want to work, or can't, are not
really equipped to give their children good mothering either.
Their babies and preschool children are malnourished or
kept closeted in dark and cheerless rooms, half-starved for
attention and affection and the necessary stimulation of
things to do and to play (work) with. For all such mothers and
children Gabe (and the Neighborhood House staff), but especially the alert, up-and-coming women of NOW, want to
provide *not* a "children's shelter," no, but a "child development center."

Now Tom gets into the act, supplementing Gabe's ideas.
What Tom knows is the resources that can be found and
tapped, financial and service resources. He knows, further,
the experiences and plans of other such centers, not only in
this city but around the country. At the center of the city's
social and health services, he knows what kind of linkages
and connections can be made between a new setup such as
Gabe suggests and already going operations. For example, he
suggests that the city Board of Health might be interested in

putting a maternal and child health clinic into the Child Care Center. And two junior colleges in the city might be interested in placing students in the Center for observation (of little children growing) and for helping in some aspects of their care. And there could be cooperation with the Board of Education which is developing a new project (suggested, incidentally, by Tom Goodwin) to continue the schooling of adolescent unwed mothers who had to drop out of school when they became pregnant. Many of them want to finish school. And those who don't still need a lot of help (in discussion groups if not in formal classes) on how to be a mother, what babies need besides bottles and diapers.

Tom pulls himself and Gabe back, laughingly, from the beautiful blueprint they're setting out. Now for some down-to-earth preliminary but necessary details. There will have to be some study on the extent of the need for a day care center in Parkside. One doesn't build a social service based only on impressions. And data must be put together on the costs involved in building, equipment, personnel. And searching inquiries into where funding might be gotten: from Washington? with some matching funds from the city, or from private foundations that might be interested in some part of the proposed program? And what will NOW be able to put in— of money-raising (if only token funds), of womanpower, of support from churches and other neighborhood organizations? Tom will bring the proposition to his board for preliminary considerations and reactions; Gabe will go forward on the groundwork with NOW. It is the beginning of building a new resource with many potential values for many children and their mothers.

Waiting for Tom in the outer office, when Gabe leaves, are two pleasant-faced middle-aged women. They are the president and the secretary of the Norshore Philanthropic League. The NPL, an organization of well-to-do women who long ago banded together for reasons of sociability and then "to do some good," came to the Community Welfare Council a little more than a year ago to ask for guidance. What should they do with the money they raised every year through a moneymaking party they'd have "just for fun"? The leaders among them (Mrs. Grey and Mrs. Rose waiting for Tom now were most vocal) had begun to question the unplanned way in which they were scattering their money grants for this and that small charity and finally had proposed to their membership that they go to the Community Welfare Council for guidance.

Tom Goodwin was assigned as their consultant. As far as he was concerned they were the answer to a prayer. Because he had a project—a sort of happy fantasy—and suddenly, in the person of a pleasantly plump and intelligent Mrs. Rose and a lean, cheerful, and competent Mrs. Grey, and all the plump, slim, intelligent, cheerful or dour, competent, and willing women they represented, he found the resources by which to make this fantasy come true.

It was a plan for old people. Tom's "specialty," as you know, is children and children's services. But, as you've already seen, social workers often have to cover the waterfront, and Tom's long interest in day care facilities for children made him seem prime for considering a "day care" facility for aged people too. That's how he got involved in working with the NPL.

For some years the social workers in the family agencies and in the recreation agencies, along with a few clergymen, had been reporting to the Community Welfare Council the increasing instances of old people who had neither the jobs, money, nor other means by which to occupy their time and their interests. A brief survey made by the research people on the Community Welfare Council staff showed that in one section of town—a neighborhood of rundown but respectable rooming houses—there was a large population of isolated aging men and women, each eking out a humble bread-and-margarine existence on pensions or relief or dwindling insurance moneys, each living in a cheerless room or two in which they ate and slept—and then looking at the dingy wallpaper. True, on spring and summer days they could walk out a bit and find a bench on which to sun themselves. But for most of the year this was not possible—and besides (as they said over and over again to the people who interviewed them), "You need someone to talk to sometimes, someone to be with, some place to go to, and something to do besides make your bed and wash your cup and saucer."

So, with the problem identified, Tom Goodwin had talked with his social worker colleagues, with the casework and group work representatives in this rooming-house area, with the interested churchmen. They had come up with the idea of developing a kind of daytime center or club in the neighborhood, specifically for old people. Here they could come for companionship, for talking together, for doing something with their hands and ears and eyes and minds, or for just sitting in a rocking chair in a cheerful airy room with other people nearby. They would, it was decided, have games— cards and checkers (or chess for the intellectuals), TV and record players, shuffleboard and ringtoss (for the athletes), craft and woodwork instruction, perhaps organized discussion groups—whether about foreign policy or adult westerns it didn't really matter, as long as these lonely, isolated people found other people to talk and listen to.

Then someone suggested that it might be nice to have a small kitchen-dining room part of such a center, so that there could be coffee time or even light lunches, so that people could eat together, because all of us, old people too, feel most sociable when joined together over food and drink. It was, in short, a fine idea, Tom and his co-planners had thought, but where to find the money to rent quarters and furnish them —and—and—and. . . . They had just about agreed on starting in a small way in one of the church basements when the NPL came along asking for guidance on how best to use its funds.

It was a solution—but, like most solutions to complex problems, not easily arrived at. Some of the women in the NPL were strongly set against the idea, didn't see the use of it; some disliked putting "all our eggs in one basket"; some had favorite charities from which they did not want to withdraw the regular grant; and so forth. This meant that Tom, as a community worker often must, took on the role of interpreter, speaker, consultant, and influencer. Even after the group had been won over and good quarters had been found there were innumerable conflicts and problems, ranging from the ridiculous to the most important, from what colors the rooms should be painted to whether the executive should be a paid social worker or a committee of volunteers. Tom was involved in many of these conflicts as well as in many of the forward-moving plans. He was again in his usual position of advising, consulting, helping to make connections and to ease communication among the many interested people involved, facilitating, enabling, supporting constructive ideas and efforts, raising "go slow" and "let's think it over" signs when questionable plans were afoot.

Mrs. Rose and Mrs. Grey are here now to drive Tom over to look at the completed, about to-be-open-for-business Senior Center. One of those gratifying moments in the life of a social worker comes when long-laid plans really work out.

If you were to remain in Tom Goodwin's office and be allowed to look into his files you'd have some idea of the other community planning and organizing projects in which he is involved, in some as a major planner, in others as an auxiliary helper. One fat folder is tabbed "School Social Work." In it are the minutes of many meetings called and given guidance by Tom on the need for social workers in the schools.

In this city, thus far, there is no money in the education budget (in part because there has been no conviction on the part of the superintendent of schools or members of the Board of Education) for a subdepartment of social workers in the schools. School social workers are needed every time a child can't make it in the school—can't learn, can't relate to his teacher or his schoolmates, can't (or won't) use the educational and social opportunities that are open to him. Teachers do not have time or space for the individual work this often takes—to talk with the child, to see his parents about what's bothering the child, often to help the child cope with problems he's having outside the school.

You will remember that schoolchildren were involved in almost all of the cases I've told you about. Mary Wright was going to talk with the teachers of Frankie Brown and the Lopez children. Don Hart was in continuous contact with the teachers of Josie Green. Moreover, he was leading a voluntary group of teachers to help them better understand the children who were their charges. Judy Foster had worked out a tutoring program for failing children with the principal and teachers of the neighborhood school. These essential social work services are not generally available for all schoolchildren. Many principals and teachers and social workers and parents think they ought to be. Thus a coalition of the PTA, interested principals, and several social agencies was formed to drive for recognition of the need for a corps of social workers hired by the Board of Education to work in the schools.

It has been a hard pull for Tom and for the committee. There is not only the opposition of the superintendent and some of his politically powerful allies in the city government but also the indifference or resistance of many school people. Add to this the rivalries among some of the PTA representatives and between them and the staffs of some schools; add to this the pulls and tugs for recognition and power in the committee. Thus, Tom, like Gabe, navigates an uneasy ship on an often stormy ocean. As a result of his patience and strategies, the "good guys" seem to be gaining on this project.

Here's another folder: "Residential Treatment for Children." That's a thin folder. Mostly it contains the documented evidence of the need for the development of "live-in" schools where seriously disturbed children can get expert treatment. Right now, in this second half of the twentieth century, state after state has no place to give care to psychotic or emotionally disturbed children except in desolate, mass-care mental hospitals, far away from their families. Often these children are thrown together in hospital wards with psychotic or deteriorated adults, living with them as "models" month after month.

Several of the child care agencies in town have begun to raise the cry for attention to these deplorable conditions. Where to find the money required? Where to find the staff expert enough in psychiatry, warm and giving enough in the everyday care of these pathetic and difficult children? That's what the "Residential Care" folder is about.

The file of folders stretches back. Each holds the notes of community projects: some finished, some just begun, some halfway along; some successful, some failures; some frustrating, some heartbreaking; some gratifying—even elating. In all of them, in small or large part, Tom Goodwin has worked with, through, and for other people. He has worked with the aim of enabling them to build a better community, helping them to put their fingers on problems and needs. He has helped them collect data that will result both in their understanding of need and in their development of plans for action. And he has tried to influence people in their relationships with one another so that they will be more cooperative than competitive, less involved in themselves alone, more concerned with the interlockings between each man and the welfare of the whole community.

Sometimes at the end of a day Tom Goodwin goes back to his small studio apartment and flops into his big leather chair (all right, imitation leather!) and wonders, "Am I building anything, really? Am I making something happen? At least, when my father puts up a building he *sees* it, standing there, concrete and steel." But most times he feels that never-ending pull, that never-ending interest in social work: the pull to see what's going to happen, what's going to become of, what next step up and out will people take if I can make those steps available to them. And sometimes, like tonight, Tom will lean back in his chair with satisfaction: one good job's done, another's begun—a good day!

It has been a long day for you, whisked from one social worker to another, to their places of work, to glimpses of their clients, their ways of working. Mary Wright, Don Hart, Judy Foster, Gabe Healy, and Tom Goodwin are all very different from one another as personalities, in their backgrounds and in their private lives. Yet they are at one, as you've seen, in their convictions about the worth and importance of human beings and about the vital importance of making human life worth the living.

There's not been time or space to introduce you to those social workers who in different capacities are active in this same over-all endeavor but who are not professionally trained. Some of them will go on to advanced training to gain the knowledge and skills that bring maximal responses with minimal trial and error. But others may not, and they will still be needed and valued. You may have caught a glimpse of what they do: José Chavez, who acts as interpreter for Mary Wright, but more than that, is a continuous "linker" between alien-feeling clients and their strange environment. The tutors in Judy Foster's program are other examples of social work aides. When the child care facility gets going there will be need not only for professional experts and volunteers but also for a corps of paid child-caring, child-teaching aides. The same holds for Tom Goodwin's Senior Center. Some of the work Gabe Healy is presently doing with the Blue Bloods and also with the young men in the work rehabilitation program could well be done by partly trained aides, supervised by Gabe, if they were available.

Professional or only partly professional ("paraprofessional" is today's word for them) social workers are bound together by the heartfelt convictions and concerns of the social work profession. Maybe this is the time to ask and answer what this profession of social work is exactly. To what do social workers "profess"?

two: What is social work?

Social work is the embodiment of our society's belief that people should have the right and the opportunity to lead personally satisfying and socially useful lives. That belief leads a society continuously to take stock of unmet human needs, of people's problems in everyday living, and of desirable personal and societal goals. This appraisal leads to the invention and development and organization of the means by which to provide for unmet social-psychological needs and to enhance people's daily social lives. This invention, development, and organization of ways and means to support and enrich people's well-being is the special occupation and preoccupation of social work.

As with every other profession, a set of values and moral principles underlies social work. Its central conviction is that each man *is* his brother's keeper and that "no man is an island unto himself." This is accompanied by the democratic tenet that since all men are not, in fact, born equal, their society owes them equality of opportunity by which to develop to their fullest potential; and sometimes it owes them extra, compensatory opportunity, to make up for their initial physical, mental, or social handicaps.

Professional social work was a long time developing, even though from earliest times people have joined together to give some form of help to their less fortunate fellow men. In the ancient temple of Jerusalem, long before the birth of Christ, the Judaic community had organized a kind of relief for the poor: a room in the temple where those citizens with surplus crops or moneys were expected to deposit their bounty unobtrusively and where the poor could come with equal anonymity to meet their needs. In medieval Europe monastic and other religious orders begged and distributed money for the poor. Sometimes, then as now, people gave money or goods or "helping hands" because it made them guilty or uncomfortable to see the suffering of others. Sometimes, then as now, they supported help to others because of some underlying fear that "there but for the grace of God go I." Sometimes they were motivated to give help and, even beyond that, to strive to prevent the causes of need by their feelings of compassion, their awareness of the interrelatedness of one man and the other.

Today even a cynic—even the man who calls himself practical or hardheaded—knows that in our complex and interlaced society what affects other men, as far away as Timbuctoo, affects him also sooner or later. One delinquent child in a schoolroom is a source of infection for other children. One bedraggled old woman searching in garbage cans for who knows what is a source of discomfort and uneasiness to all who pass her by. One family whose children show the scars of want or brutality is a festering sore on the body of the community.

Thus, out of many different personal motives, all of which had to do with man's relationship to man, and out of religious and social ideals that emphasized man's obligations to his fellow man, there developed certain organized aids to people who lacked the means to buy food and clothing and shelter or carry out the ordinary activities of everyday life. In the United States (where social services are most fully developed) as late as the last century these organized aids were chiefly food and clothing handouts, sometimes money grants, sometimes—for some special occasion like Christmas or Thanksgiving—a gift basket which held the cheerful glow of an orange or the glint of a toy in addition to the drab staples that flesh and bone required.

Old records in family service agencies early in the twentieth century carry entries like this: "Visited the H family, all in bed to keep warm. Because of the bitter cold last week's coal had been used up. Left $3 for coal. ..." "Mr. G said he had not been able to work this week because his horse died. His family has been refused credit at the grocery store. There is no food or fuel in the house. He asks for $25 to buy a horse so he can resume his peddling." You may be sure that in those days that request would have had to come up for consideration by a board before it was granted. Twenty-five dollars in cash was considered a sobering sum to entrust to a poor man, even as late as the twentieth century.

But the board that would consider whether to buy Mr. G a bony nag to pull his rickety wagon was already, mind you, a group of people who were concerned not only with putting one day's or one week's food into the hungry mouths of Mr. G's children but, beyond this, with helping Mr. G to maintain his self-supporting activities. They were already interested not just in getting rid of Mr. G with a handout but in prevent-

ing economic breakdown, in building up Mr. G's initiative as
a breadwinner. In this sense they and the caseworkers were
the forerunners of modern social work.

From earliest times in this country, too, another type of
organized aid developed. This was the provision of shelters
or institutions to care for men, women, and children with all
manner of troubles and needs. Some of these were hospitals
patterned after those in Europe, where the poor who were
sick and disabled—young, old, men, women, children, physically sick, mentally sick, pregnant, dying—were clapped together to be given shelter and subsistence out of the way of
the sturdy members of the community. (It took a long time
before a hospital came to be thought of as a desirable place
to go to when one was sick, and among some groups, for
whom stories of those nineteenth-century hospitals were
vivid, there still remains the idea that "a hospital is where
you go to die"!) Other kinds of institution were orphanages,
where full orphans, part orphans, abandoned children,
foundlings were all herded together. (Dickens' *Oliver Twist*
gives a vivid picture of one of these dreary and dreadful
places, and it served to alert many good people to conditions
they scarcely knew of as they went about their own ordered
and secure lives.) And there were the asylums and alms-
houses: the one where mentally sick and mentally deficient
people were cast into wretched oblivion; the other where
people who could not make a living were given a dirty corner
to sleep in and a daily ration of bread.

All these were organizations set up for two purposes: First,
to rid the community of its sick and poor and dependent and
misfit people, so that these "lesser" human beings should not
interfere with the welfare of its more fortunate citizens. The
second purpose was to provide some means by which life,

and then life with some decency, and then life with some open opportunity, might be sustained. Little by little these later purposes became the primary ones of such organizations. Social reformers spearheaded this movement from the "handout" to the "buildup"; from viewing the poor and the sick as "les misérables" to seeing each person as a human being with human feelings and potentials; from providing meager shelter and food to providing a whole range of opportunities by which even the poor and the sick and the emotionally disturbed or otherwise handicapped human being could live in the community, go to school, work, have and hold a family, get medical care, find some recreation. These reformers made it their progressive mission to change social institutions so that they would truly meet human needs and enhance human life. Many of these reformers were clergymen, writers, physicians; others, not part of a profession then recognized, took the name "social workers."

The social workers of the nineteenth and the early twentieth centuries were volunteers, both men and women. For some of them social work was a time filler, an avocational and "worthy" pursuit. Some of them were people with good hearts who wanted to be helpful to others. Some were people with grim consciences who wanted to reform others. Some, once they saw living conditions in slums or medical conditions in hospitals or working conditions in sweatshops, caught fire and burned with indignation at the social conditions that ground out the humanness in men. From among all of these—the dabblers, the earnest, and the dedicated ones —there rose a small but staunch body of people who combined compassionate human feelings with sturdy social concerns, who had intellectual curiosity and vigor, and whose grasp of social problems and social needs was accompanied by vision about ways by which these needs might be met and problems prevented. Some of these men and women were giants: Arnold Toynbee, the uncle of the historian, Dorothea Dix, Samuel Gridley Howe, and Josephine Shaw Lowell are only a few among them. They and their like and all the hard-working but forgotten ones who fervently believed along with them that the welfare of each human being is the purpose and the test of a society—they were the forerunners and the shapers of modern social work.

You can imagine that if they came back today they would scarcely believe the changes that have occurred in American society, in our social philosophy, in social work, and in social workers. They would be astounded to find that welfare is now big business. They would find that many kinds of deteriorating sicknesses and permanent handicaps are being covered by great governmental insurance systems. Prevention of poverty and sickness is part of the program; and for such problems as have already occurred, state and town as well as the federal government offer financial help, medical care, and various forms of child welfare assistance. They would find a tremendous network of privately supported welfare agencies too—family agencies, psychiatric clinics and hospitals, child guidance clinics, child care agencies—a bewildering range of ways and means to meet people's varied needs. If they struck up a conversation with the proverbial man in the street they might find him worried that we were becoming a "welfare state." They might be naïve enough to ask him what was wrong with that: Would a "misery state" be preferable? And then they would find that the word "welfare" had become loaded with all kinds of emotions and misconceptions, but that in the last analysis even this worrier about welfare believed in the right of the individual to life with decency, liberty, and at least some opportunity to pursue happiness.

Perhaps one of the things that would surprise the nineteenth-century social worker most (after he got over his shock at all our new inventions and changed styles and standards of living!) would be how our ideas of human need have changed. In his day it was assumed that the full stomach made a whole man. Today, for many reasons too complex to be gone into here, we have become keenly aware that man does not live by bread alone. Our ideas of what we want for ourselves and for others, in terms of psychological and social as well as physical well-being, have developed with all the rapidity and intensity of other twentieth-century ideas. We believe that a family needs not only a roof over its head and food for its nurture but good, healthy relationships among its members. We have become concerned that marriages should hold and should be gratifying to husband and wife, that children should be "understood" and helped to unfold their full potentials of mind and personality, that people should find their occupations and their relationships with others rewarding and enhancing to their lives—and so forth. So it is that the kinds of social service and the ways of helping people have developed far beyond what pioneer social workers would have dreamed of. And they would probably look with amazement at the kinds of problems that Don Hart and Gabe Healy and the other social workers you've met are dealing with, and with astonishment at the resources they are able to command, and at their knowledge of man-in-his-society which informs their helping skills.

Funny thing about people: they continuously strive to be or to get more or better than they have. There is something inborn in the human spirit, especially in an open society, that pushes for self-actualization. So that when one level of well-

being has been achieved people look up, higher, wanting and
expecting something better for themselves. The more affluent a society (and ours is probably the most affluent the world
has ever known) the more people's level of expectancy for
themselves and their children rises. Once basic bread-and-
butter needs are met, people begin to feel that they need
opportunities beyond those of material welfare. They want
and need educational and recreational opportunities, better
housing, more interesting or more rewarding jobs, and so on.
What in some societies would be considered sheer luxury—
a refrigerator, for instance—is in our society considered a
basic necessity. When, not too long ago, the poor in our society simply took it for granted that when high school was
completed their children went to work, today's poor want
and expect their children to have college opportunities. (One
reads a great deal these days about the "culture of the poor"
as different from "middle-class values." But stop and ask any
poor man and woman whether they like their "culture" or
not, and what they aspire to have, and you'll find that the
answer to the first is essentially "no" and the answer to the
second is that they aspire to the life opportunities valued by
the middle class!) The point is this: that only an affluent society supports a broad program of social services, financially
and attitudinally. And that social services and social work
grow rather than diminish as there grows a rising valuation
of human life and a rising standard of human rights.

Along with this increased and widespread belief in man's
rights to self-fulfillment and in his accompanying responsibility for the welfare of his fellow man there has occurred what
is practically an explosion of knowledge about the nature of
man and his social organizations (from the family outward)
and also knowledge about ways by which men are hindered

or helped in their struggle for selfhood and competence. These knowledges and skills do not just come naturally; they must be learned and practiced. Their use must be safeguarded by certain ethical principles and sanctioned by the community that supports them. So social work, once the practice of anyone who wanted to "do good," has now become a profession.

That means, first of all, that it has marked off a particular area of human living as its area of concern and expertness. Social welfare, yours and mine, is the concern of a great number of professions. Education, medicine, engineering, the ministry, law are all concerned with individual and societal welfare. Each one concentrates on some particular aspect of human well-being, and at points each may overlap another profession. The profession of social work has areas that overlap medicine, psychiatry, law, education, recreational work, and so on. But its particular and special concern is with enabling people, singly or in groups, to work and love and live together in ways that build their sense of human dignity and social responsibility.

The aim of social work, then, is to restore, reinforce, or re-form the efforts people make to cope with their problems or achieve their desirable goals, and to restore, reinforce, or re-form their environmental conditions and resources to meet common human needs.

That's a big order. To bulwark this concern, commitment, and aim, then, social work, like other professions, must have a basic philosophy or guiding belief; a body of knowledge about its area of concern and operation; certain skills and processes by which it translates that knowledge into action; and organized resources. Its practitioners—whether they be group workers, caseworkers, community workers, research-

ers, administrators, they are social workers all—are selected
for their personal and intellectual ability to master the subject matter, to put their knowledge to use, and to identify
with and be guided by the values and ethics of the profession.
They are paid for their work, and they are committed to
service and to advancement of the common good.

Does this sound ponderous and overwhelming? Perhaps
some brief explanations and examples will give it life.

You may already have realized, as you watched Don Hart
and Mary Wright and the others, that they were working not
just "by hunch and by golly" but by insights into the psychology of people they were dealing with. They were "tuned
in" on what people were feeling and thinking, and that is
what made them able to be helpful. Moreover, they had a
grasp of what causes problems, what resources can be pulled
in to deal with them, how needs differ from one person to
another, and how treatment needs to be differentiated. You
may have noted the skill they used in the ways they related
to people and how they tried to bring out the best potentials
in each person whose life they touched. These operations
and the knowledge underlying them were studied and
learned as part of their professional education.

You may have been aware, too, of how self-disciplined
these trained social workers were. This is a major mark of a
profession: that its practitioners are committed to using
themselves in the service of others. A professional social
worker must be aware and in control of his own needs and
drives so that they do not get between him and the person
he is trying to help. Of course this is not only a kind of ethical
attitude, but makes good common sense too, because people
are best empowered to work on their problems when their
own motors are set running, not when they've been pushed

or towed by the motor of someone else. Yet it is hard, this discipline and management of what you feel and what you'd like to have happen, when your client is being difficult or unreasonable in the many ways people have of being unreasonable. Perhaps this is one of the main differences between the person who just happens into social work or even the dedicated volunteer of earlier days and today's professional worker: that the professional has been trained to be self-aware and alert to the fact that it is not *his* feelings and drives that are to be gratified, but rather those of the person he is to help.

Along with other professions, social work has a basic code of ethics and a system of values which its practitioners profess. Among its fundamental beliefs are these:

It affirms the sanctity of human life and therefore the dignity of every human being. By "dignity" we mean the inner push in every person to get up on his own two feet, to be seen and accepted by others as a creature of worth, as one who is like his fellow men and yet is his individual self also.

In their many different ways social workers try to uphold or reinforce the human dignity of people who are struggling against odds that sometimes demean them or lower their self-respect. They work to restore the sense of selfhood in people who have "given up"—an alcoholic, for instance, or the father of a family who throws in the sponge and deserts after months of unsuccessful job hunting. Acting on their belief in each man's worth, social workers attempt to bring about changes in society's appraisal of and attitudes toward certain outcast people—for example, to create understanding that the woman who has a baby out of wedlock is not necessarily evil or deserving of punishment. Social workers hold it to be true, even of the person who seems to have become worthless to himself and his society, that as long as there is life in him there is also some flicker of aspiration to do or to be better than he is.

Another conviction in social work is the right of each person to self-determination, to be master of his own fate. This means that a person has the right to make his own choices as to what he will do and be. Practically, however, one's choices may be sharply limited by lack of means or opportunity. Social workers try to broaden the scope of opportunities for their clients. Practically, too, you can't freely choose what you will have or do or be unless you consider what the consequences of that decision will be for you and for others whose welfare is bound up with yours. Therefore, much of the social worker's efforts goes into helping individuals and groups to consider carefully the pros and cons of the actions they wish to take or avoid. The very process of this mulling over and thinking through, whether it occurs in one of Judy Foster's groups or in one of Tom Goodwin's committees, develops in people considered and thoughtful ways by which to make personal or communal decisions.

Self-determination is also limited by the rights of others. Social workers try to help people to achieve maximum freedom of choice and self-expression with the provisos that such choice will have constructive consequences and that such freedom does not infringe upon the rights and freedoms of other people.

Sometimes social workers are caught in conflict as to where the rights of an individual leave off and his responsibilities to others or to the group take over. To help deal with this problem is another basic idea: that the person and his society are interdependent, that each takes from the other, each "owes" the other. Thus social workers formulate their aims in terms of helping people to lead personally satisfying *and* socially useful lives; and when they look at society at large they say that the purpose and test of a good society is the welfare of the individual.

Another basic value which social workers profess is that of "joint participation." This means that a person or family or group is recognized as not only having the "right" to make its own decisions about its own problems and solutions but also is recognized as having the "power" to do so, provided that "power" is brought to life or is released and appropriately channeled. This is based not only on respect for other people but on a plain and simple fact that social workers have long observed: when people are active in their own behalf, when they have a partnership in a plan rather than being only a receiver of someone else's plan, they are much more likely to make it work. Participation means the deposit of one's self in a partnership to get something done. This is why social workers—whether a caseworker working with one person or a community worker dealing with a committee—operate always to put the "client" in the driver's seat. The social worker may provide the gas, maybe even step on the starter, and he will advise on the road map. But the driver holds the power to stop or go, to go fast or slowly, to take or reject road suggestions or advice. The point is that when he achieves his nearby or far-off goal he must have the rewarding and self-enhancing feeling that he's been an active agent, he's had some part and power in bringing about the change he has wanted.

A profession offers its services not only through the knowledge and skills of its individual practitioners but through certain organized institutions which "bank" its wisdom, experience, and resources. Lawyers have a legal system and courts, doctors their hospitals and clinics and laboratories, teachers the school system, ministers the church. The laboratories and banked experience and organized resources and provisions of the profession of social work are social agencies. (For more about them, see Chapter Four.)

Social agencies are the employers of social workers. So are social service departments of other kinds of human welfare agencies, such as hospitals and vocational rehabilitation centers and schools. Social workers are hired by social agencies to carry their services into action. As such each social worker on the job represents, to his client, to the community, to the public, his agency in action. Sometimes young people do not fully take in this fact, and nurture some idea that they will be "free-lance" social workers, operating on their own, particularly since "social agency" implies some sort of "establishment." At present the only free-lance social workers are caseworkers (and a few group workers) whose years of good clinical experience and agency supervision qualify them for private therapeutic practice. But even these, when they act responsibly, get their sanction from their professional organization, the National Association of Social Workers.

As in teaching, the ministry, engineering, and some other professions, there is sometimes a conflict between the fact of being both the employee of an established institution and a professional. The fact is that without social workers an agency is largely a blueprint. Social workers are the agency in action. The further fact is that without professional social workers agencies might become rigid, mechanized bureaucracies. So the professional social worker, a carrier of ethical commitments, standards, and values, with knowledge of social problems and the better rather than worse ways of dealing with them, is expected to be an agency changer and builder.

As a profession social work is involved not only in finding
and providing resources for people's social well-being but
also with constantly studying, evaluating, and re-forming the
resources and services and methods it (or other forces in the
community) has already developed. As such, the profession
aims to be not merely a deliverer of services but an instrument of social change. On his part the individual professional
social worker is expected, not too long after he earns his
master's degree, to undertake and carry leadership positions
in social work. Opportunities for leadership—whether in the
skills of clinical practice or as supervisor of other social workers, in administration, in training paraprofessionals, in
demonstrating and experimenting with new and special
agency projects—are not only open to the professionally educated social worker, they are literally thrust upon him. The
professional social worker should be his profession's severest
critic as well as its staunchest spokesman and representative.
If in his professional judgment an agency's policies or programs or processes are contrary to or obstacles to the social
work profession's values and commitments, his professional
responsibility is to make this known and to take some appropriate steps toward needed change. There will be many conflicts for him, between what *is* and what he believes *should
be,* between settling for "it's good because we've always
done it this way" and questioning "is it done this way because it's actually been found to be good?" This question is
increasingly being asked by social workers and in part it
accounts for the greatly increased interest in research in
social work practice.

As a profession social work is very young. Until well into
the second decade of this century most of what was called
social work was under voluntary auspices and its practitioners were volunteers or poorly paid "agents." The oldest

schools of social work, such as those at the University of
Chicago and Columbia University are little more than fifty
years old. It was less than fifty years ago that the first such
school became part of the graduate school complex in a university. Today there are in the United States and Canada
more than seventy accredited graduate schools of social
work. Some of them are chiefly concerned with the preparation and production of competent professional manpower.
Others, along with them, are making substantial contributions to social work's research and the development and organization of its body of knowledge. From these scholarly
efforts as well as from skilled practice a profession grows and
gains stature.

Youthfulness, whether in a person or a profession, has
many advantages. It is characterized by vigor, buoyancy,
growth potential, flexibility. It has some disadvantages too, as
every young person knows. The young are less likely to command the respect of their elders; they are often open to
critical questioning especially when they break with tradition; and, one must admit it, they are often unsure of their
identity, they tend to be "all over the place," "into everything." The comparative youth of social work as a profession
shares these advantages and disadvantages. Its separate identity from some other human welfare endeavors—social psychiatry, education, civil rights organizations, for example—is
not always clear and sharp. There is considerable overlap
with these and other such human welfare services especially
in the present period when every week sees the pop-up of
some new venture or project to ensure the well-being of
people and community life.

I suppose it may be said that one mark of the professional
social worker is his ability to tolerate uncertainty and even,

at times, ambiguity. This is not just a personal capacity. It is built in by professional knowledge of social work's history, of the expectable impact of social change upon social institutions, including professions, and so on. (Even medicine, that entrenched and hallowed profession, is experiencing considerable internal questioning and shake-up these days.)

But the professional social worker has several anchorages. One lies in what he knows, not just what he has experienced but the explanations and interpretations and systematic organizations of experience; another is in his "know-how," not just his natural skill, but again his firm grasp of the principles that govern what to do when. Another anchorage is his agency, if it is a professionally directed one. Another is in the code of ethics and values that are part of the professional social worker's "oath" and commitment. This code, along with other standards, has been developed within the National Association of Social Workers, professional social work's membership association which today numbers almost 50,000 (including special student membership). Through its national committees and its local chapters the National Association of Social Workers deals with all kinds of problems: those that have to do with the social worker himself, such as his operation within the profession's ethical codes or such as salary and agency practices; and those that concern the advancement of the profession, such as the development of standards of competence; and those that have to do with promoting action on social issues, such as testifying and lobbying for or against legislation that bears on social welfare.

When you read this the National Association of Social Workers membership may have made some decisions that will signally affect the profession of social work for the future. As I write this there is a ballot on my desk—and on that of

the 49,999 other members of the National Association of
Social Workers—asking for a yea or nay vote on the issue of
whether to admit into associate membership persons who
have only a bachelor's degree, providing they are in the
employment of some social welfare agency and provided that
they have taken a block of relevant courses in the undergraduate social work curriculum. This has a lot to do with you,
in case you want to enter social work or be a social worker
right after college. So I must say something here about how
the profession of social work is turning to consider the need
for and usefulness of what are called "paraprofessionals"
(which means *"akin* to" or "by the side of" the professional).
Sometimes they are called social work aides. (You caught
some glimpses of them working alongside the social workers
I introduced you to in Chapter One.) Sometimes they are
named "technicians." Medicine, dentistry, nursing, psychiatry have all used and are increasingly using aides or technicians or paraprofessionals to carry some aspects of their
services. The need for the profession of social work to do so
was never greater because there is simply not enough professional manpower to cover the tremendous proliferation of
social services that are being asked for today.

Social work, then, as a profession and within many kinds
of agencies has turned to two jobs: first, to figure out what
kinds of services can be given by paraprofessionals, people
whose interests and personalities and partial training enable
them to take the place of or to supplement the work of professional caseworkers, group workers, and community workers;
second, what kind of course work or on-the-job training
would benefit such aides and helpers.

One of the arguments for the admission of people with a
B.A. degree (and with social work courses) into the National

Association of Social Workers membership is that hundreds upon hundreds of them are already "in" social work. Most of the "relief investigators" or "caseworkers" in the public assistance agencies or in many public child welfare agencies have never had professional training. Yet they are called "social workers." Actually their great visibility to the public eye has been one of the reasons for public confusion as to what a professional social worker is or what the profession of social work is.

And that leads to still another argument for the profession's recognition of the vast army of social service "aides" and "technicians" that is presently at work, and growing, and necessary for coverage of social welfare needs. It is that social work as a profession will, at best, be forced to identify more clearly what its particular areas of knowledge, expertise, and responsibility are and to concentrate upon their development.

(If you want to know more about how to be a social worker without full professional training, see Chapters Five and Seven.)

As you can see, "what is social work" is not easily explained. Partly this is because it is a rapidly expanding field of work. And partly it is that it has to do with so many aspects of complex human beings in complicated social transactions. In a nutshell it may be said (again) that social work is a profession (and occupation) devoted to the restoration or the reinforcement or the re-forming of social opportunities and resources, and simultaneously to the restoration, reinforcement, and re-forming of the efforts of individual people and groups to make fullest use of the resources in themselves and those in their social environment. That's a mouthful. But so is anything that deals with people-in-social-situations.

Having chewed on that—and thinking back to the social workers you saw in action in Chapter One—you may pose another question and wish for another encapsulated answer. What, exactly, do social workers *do?* In order to restore, reinforce, re-form, how would I be operating if I were to be a social worker? That's what the next chapter is about.

three: **What do**
social workers do?

In order to restore, reinforce, or re-form the social functioning of individuals and groups, social workers must work for,
with, and through people. There are no switches to pull or
gadgets to push in social work. (Sometimes weary social workers wish there were!) There are only people.

There are the people who have problems and need help
with them. There are the people who, by their actions or
attitudes, make those problems better or worse. There are
people who can provide help and people who, by their position and power, control circumstances that when bad create
"social need" and when good constitute "social opportunity." Sometimes social workers talk of dealing with people
and their environments, but when you take a good hard look
at it you'll see that, except for weather, natural objects, and
the artifacts with which we surround ourselves, the environment that is important to us is made up of people—their
actions, attitudes, and the organized operations they create
and run. Our "social environment" is made up largely of

people, and social workers work with, for, and through these
people too.

Social workers help clients with all the kinds of social problems you can think of. They help parents with problems in
relation to their children and children with problems in relation to their parents; they counsel husbands and wives who
have marital conflicts; they place children in foster or adoptive homes when their parents cannot care for them; they
help the patients of doctors and psychiatrists to find ways of
managing their daily lives in spite of physical and emotional
handicaps; they help adolescents and young adults find
themselves and what they want to do with themselves. They
help people in crises caused by loss of wages, by death, or by
sudden illness, and they help people with problems in their
social relationships which have been festering for many
years.

You saw a number of these problems in the cases carried
by Mary Wright and Don Hart, and some of them lurked
under the surface in Judy Foster and Gabe Healy's groups of
youngsters.

Whatever the problems that are brought for help to social
workers (whether caseworkers or group workers) the help
that is given is of three main kinds.

The first of these is compassionate understanding of the
person who's in trouble, understanding of him as a hurt and,
at the moment, helpless person, and then understanding of
him in relation to the problem he's suffering. "Compassionate
understanding" means, of course, that one conveys the sense
that "I *feel* with you. I not only see you and hear you and take
in what you're saying but I can feel into your hurt" (or despair
or anger, whatever the person's feeling is). If you yourself
have ever been in trouble and haven't known how to deal

with it you will know how another person's compassionate understanding can be the first step in feeling "helped."

The second kind of help is guidance and counseling in problem solving. This involves a whole complex of processes and interchanges between the social worker and his client over time, but it may be characterized as a talking over and considering and feeling through and thinking over how best or better to cope with the problem.

The third major kind of help for people with problems is that of providing or making accessible to them the kinds of practical aids, tangible material resources, or services that they do not have or cannot command.

Some cases need all of these; some need one more than another. Take Mrs. Black, for instance, the woman who came to Don Hart for placement of her aged father. Mrs. Black first thought she needed only a material resource: a *place* to put her father. But what quickly became evident was that she needed psychological help in working out the emotional conflicts that this "solution" had raised in her. And it goes without saying that her freedom to talk out her feelings with Don was based on the sense he conveyed of understanding her and her problem empathically. So she needed all three characteristic kinds of casework help. Take the Soul Queens, Judy Foster's group of young adolescents. They wanted the material resources offered them by the Neighborhood House —a room to dance in, a kitchen to fix hot dogs and fries in, a place to socialize. But at times of conflict or confusion in their group relationships they wanted Judy's guidance in ways to resolve it. And at times of real trouble—as with their member who became pregnant—they looked to Judy for several kinds of help: compassionate understanding first, then guidance and advice, and steering to places where services relating to the problem could be had.

Increasingly over the past few years social workers have been thinking not only of how to deal with present problems but also about how to *prevent* sociopsychological problems from developing. So they work at building up resources and opportunities toward the prevention of people's difficulties or breakdown. Thus Gabe Healy draws a group of actual or potential delinquents into the Neighborhood House in an effort to engage and channel their wants and energies in constructive directions to *prevent* delinquency. Moreover, he has his eye on several of them whom he hopes to help not only to avoid trouble but to realize and maximize their apparent capacities. Thus Mary Wright, when she plans to report the paint and plaster condition in Mrs. Brown's tenement to the Tenants' Organization, is bound on *prevention,* not only for the Browns' little Frankie but for all the occupants of that building. Thus Tom Goodwin, working with the Norshore Philanthropic League to establish a Senior Center, was looking to *prevent* the kinds of loneliness and consequent psychological and physical breakdowns that occur in aged people.

Each day social workers deal with people who have problems in their daily person-to-person or person-to-environment living and also with people (often they're the same people) who need and want better chances to stretch and expand their potentials and experiences. Beyond this they work to influence the people who constitute their clients' "environment"—with teachers of children having school troubles, for instance, with family members who are involved (like Clayton's mother) with (at a broader and higher echelon level) persons whose decisions affect large groups of other people (such as the Board of Education and the decisions it will make about school social workers). Actually all "social action," all changes in the laws or provisions for social change, take place through influencing the attitudes and consequent actions of key people.

This is easier said than done. People do not change their behavior and attitudes toward others just because it's explained to them that they ought to or that it would be good for the other person if they did so. Mothers, teachers, landlords, friends, doctors—all of us—have our own feelings and desires too, and it often takes a good deal of discussion and "working through" before these attitudes and motives are changed. Social workers do a great deal of their work, then, with and through the people around their clients who, by what they do and say, make the clients' lives better or worse.

In addition to the client's family and some of the other people he is associated with—employers, fellow workers, neighbors—there are many professional people whose actions may bear upon his welfare. Doctors, visiting nurses, courts with their judges, lawyers, or probation officers—these and other kinds of professional people are drawn by social workers into the orbit of planning for a client. The social worker's efforts with them are the coordination of what they are doing, the joint understanding of the person or family's particular needs and particular feelings, and the joint agreements on how to help most effectively.

Last, there are those people who come together voluntarily —members of agency boards or of a neighborhood association—who wish to provide some necessary service to the community or to meet some present problem. It might be a problem troubling the group itself—such as bad housing which sparked the formation of the Parkside Tenants' Organization. Or it might be a problem that holds some special interest and gratification for the group, as the Senior Center did for the NPL. Or it might be a combination of the two, as it was for the members of NOW, some of whom wanted a day care center to meet their own needs for child care and some of whom wanted it because they thought it was a socially desirable thing to have in Parkside. Any one of these groups may call upon social workers—caseworkers, group workers, or community workers, as you've seen—for consultation, guidance, certain kinds of knowledge or perspectives based on social work knowledge and experience. Here, too, social workers work with, for, and through people.

When you stop to think of it, there is a very wide and broad "peopled" area that social workers deal with, from individuals torn apart by personal problems, to families suffering chronic illness and chronic poverty, to individuals and groups wanting some better life and some greater opportunities than they have, to individuals and groups who want aid and guidance in how to provide such opportunities, to individuals and groups whose actions and attitudes impede progress or even actually create the problematic conditions that exist. It's a big order. This is why it has been necessary for social work to develop certain general principles that govern the ways social workers do what they do. These hold whether the social work method being used is casework, group work, or community work. It is these general ways of procedure that I shall try to explain in what follows. (There will be exceptions to all these "rules" of action, of course. But by and large they describe the ways by which people are helped to deal with their problems whether "the problem" is something to be got rid of or is a problem of how to build.)

(1). *The social worker starts by indicating that he wants to understand the problem:* What's up—what's the trouble—what's the person's picture of the difficulty or proposal he's concerned with?

"To understand" as has been said, means more than "to get it into my head." In social work it means to take in something not only intellectually but feelingly, to take in both the objective and the subjective meanings of a person's—or a community's—problems. So the social worker lends himself sensitively to drawing out and hearing what the problem carrier or the person reporting it says. People's problems have a way of sounding as if they were the same thing when they are simply called by familiar names—"delinquency," "marital discord," "poverty," "bad housing," "no recreational facilities," and so on. But the social worker knows that only one generalization can be made about problems. That is that every problem is different from every other one. It is different either in the elements that go to make it up or in the way it affects the particular people who have it. Therefore, a professional social worker doesn't conclude that one unmarried mother is just like another or that bad housing is causing delinquency. Rather he gives himself over to finding out exactly what the particular facts of a particular situation are.

2. *The social worker gets the objective and subjective facts of the problem:* The objective facts of a problem are manifold, of course, but generally they consist of identifying what it is, how it got that way, who and what is harmed by it, what has been done to try to deal with it, what has and hasn't worked, and why. In an individual person's problem one or two interviews may reveal the necessary facts to start some action on the problem. In a community's problem it may be necessary to do a study to ascertain "the facts," such as when Tom Goodwin and Gabe Healy agreed that facts of need had to be established before full plans could be launched for a day care center.

Subjective facts are those facts of the feelings that the

problem arouses, or sometimes the feelings that cause the problem, and the consequent ways the person views his problem, himself, and others in relation to it. Social workers know that the way people feel about and perceive their problems has a great deal to do with what they will be willing and able to do about them. They know that the best-laid plans and the finest solutions will fall flat if the people for whom they are made have had no part in making them or if they do not want them. They know that people mature and gain self-reliance as their potential capacities to think through a problem are drawn out and exercised; and that only as people are helped to express and deal with their distress and anxiousness and prejudices and angers will they be free enough to see straight and think clearly.

Thus the social worker works to ascertain and understand the person's feelings about the problem, the ways he is involved in it, his wishes and needs, his thinking about it and its solution, his willingness and capacity to grapple with it, what other people in his immediate life situation do to affect him, badly or well, and so forth. Our clients are like ourselves. When someone shows us he is interested not only in what our problem is but also in our own personal, individual reaction to it, in how we see it, feel it, interpret it—then, and only then, do we feel personally understood. When we have been allowed or, more, encouraged to express ourselves, not just our ideas, an interesting human experience occurs. We feel related to, connected with, the person who has drawn us out and heard us out.

3. *The social worker develops a vital, sustaining, and working relationship with his client:* "Relationship" is a subject that could fill a book and still remain elusive and hard to capture in words because it is something like "love"—more

to be experienced than expressed in words. As it is used in social work a professional relationship means that one is related to a client for a purpose, and that purpose is problem solving of some sort. But it is recognized that people in trouble often need to feel the support and sustainment of another sturdy and warmly interested person.

People who are under stress of problems or troubles or people who are reaching out for new experiences feel released and empowered when another person who seems steady and trustworthy indicates that he is with them. All of us gain inner strength and security from good relationships with people we respect and trust. Not all of us have such people standing by when we most need them. Social workers know the importance of borrowing strength from another, of feeling surer because a person who is likable shows that he likes you. They know that the emotional linkage of good relationships can nourish and sustain people through crises and over long stretches of difficulty.

Therefore, from the very first day of his training, the social worker is kept aware of the importance of warmth and acceptance in promoting human growth, of being "client-centered" and managing to control his own subjectivities, of using himself in such ways as to say in effect, "I am *with* you and I am *for* you. I am *with* you in my acceptance of your feelings. I am *for* you to help you find some better way to be, or act, or work out your problem."

It is easy to see how a warm and caring and sustaining relationship would be a tremendous factor in getting Mrs. Brown and Mrs. Lopez to trust and work along with Mary Wright, in moving Josie Green to believe in herself because her caseworker, Don Hart, believed in her, in binding the Soul Queens to Judy Foster and making what she thought and said matter to them. But even the "clients" of Gabe Healy and Tom Goodwin who are often "powers" in the community want and need not "tenderness" or "caring," perhaps, but someone they feel they can trust, depend on, and someone they feel is at one with them in their problem-solving efforts. There are times, many times, in work with community blocs and groups when the social worker must control his personal biases and feelings and give himself over to the needs and drives of group members with steadiness and interest so they will feel connected *with* him rather than pitted *against* him. (This doesn't mean that the social worker must go along with the other person's ideas or acts. It means that he accepts and understands the motives and feelings that underlie them—he accepts the *person*, though not necessarily his plan or behavior. Thus, when Tom Goodwin must "fight" for social work in the schools, he fights *for* the idea and *against* opposing ideas but he continues to relate to the principals with the attention and respect for their rights and positions that win their reciprocal respect for him.) Of course relationship is of particular importance when the social worker's client is troubled and hurt.

4. Within the sustaining relationship *the social worker helps his client to recognize and express the feelings that hamper him* or stand in the way of his adequate functioning. When people have difficult problems, they are often so full of anxiety or guilt or white-hot anger or black-cold despair that they cannot do anything but try to keep the lid on their emotions. Their feelings paralyze them or rise like clouds before their eyes and keep them from seeing straight or clearly. Then their actions in relation to their problems are likely to be poorly planned or even inappropriate. Social workers understand all this and therefore they always attend

to what and how people are feeling. They help people to speak out, to express their emotions, and by their acceptance and talking these feelings over (sometimes over and over and over again!) they help to dilute or even radically change them, and thus change the person's slant on his problem and his behavior.

This happens all the time in casework: caseworkers need to help people know and work over the emotions that crowd in on them and complicate their problems. It often happens in group work, when the feelings and consequent behavior of one member of a group skews the group's activities and relationships. Then the group worker knows he has to pay particular attention or give particular help to the one or several persons who are emotionally disturbed and disturbing. And it is not at all unusual for people who are working with a community worker, ostensibly to give service to others, to become quite emotionally upset and involved. The social worker does not in any sense begin to "treat" them; but he will surely have to find out from them what's behind their grim determination to do this or that, their violent prejudice about him or her, their opposition to one or another plan.

Supporting his clients by his warmth and concern and/or acceptance and respect, within the bonds of a purposeful relationship,

5. *The social worker sizes up the problem,* its import, the persons and conditions that are involved in it, either as problem sufferers or problem solvers (and sometimes this is the same person). In short, he *makes an assessment or diagnosis.* This is an appraisal not only of what the problem is and what it needs for its solution or modification but also of what powers of motivation and capability can be called forth in the person himself by which he can deal with it. And also what

aids and resources exist in the environment—personal, familial, communal—that can be utilized to meet or modify the problem. Then the social worker sets about mobilizing these. But always together with the wish and will and efforts of his client.

6. *The social worker keeps his client working as an active participant* in clarifying the problem, his relationship to it, his assessment of it, and his wishes and ideas as to what to do about it. The reasons for this you already know.

But this is more easily said than done! Sometimes people are so tired out or discouraged by their problems that they want someone else to take all responsibility for them. Some people—delinquents, for example—may not see their own need for help and are not sure anyhow that they can trust anyone with their innermost feelings. Some people want a ready-made solution in a neat package and are impatient with exploring the facts ("Don't bother me with the facts— I've got my mind made up!"). Each of these kinds of person calls for a different psychological approach by the social worker. But behind the differences of technique is the governing idea that what a person works out for himself is most likely to be acted on by him because it is *his*.

It would be simple, for example, for Judy Foster to say to the Soul Queens, "Now the way to have a nice party is to do this, that, and the other," and, depending on their mood, they might say, "Yeah, okay, great"—and then go about the thing halfheartedly or with a dejected sense that this wasn't their party at all. Instead she said, "Let's think and talk about how you can make it fun, what do you want to happen, how will it come out if you do this—or that. . . ." The "problem solving" was theirs. Moreover, they learned from it a way of going about making their own thought-out decisions. It would be easy for Mary Wright to say, "Look, Mrs. Brown, a child can't be slapped out of being afraid. That doesn't make sense." And Mrs. Brown, out of her respect for authority, might have said, "All right. I'll stop hitting Frankie." But she'd be no further along with knowing what to do with him. So Mary Wright took the long way around—which, as the proverb says, is often the shortest way home. First to let Mrs. Brown know that she felt with *her*. Then she would begin (with Mr. Brown present) to exercise their own efforts to wonder why Frankie "acts bad," why he's afraid, what might help him, how do they suppose it is that a child will keep on doing what he knows is bad for him—and so on. Mr. and Mrs. Brown will by this active thinking and wondering and guessing together with Mary Wright be enhanced in their capacity to be parents, because parent feelings and parent thinking have been exercised.

7. All through their work together *the social worker supports and exercises his client's own powers of motivation, thought, and action.* This means that along with talking over "how I feel," the client is stimulated to consider, together with the social worker, "what I think about these feelings, what I think about my behavior, my problems, and the reasons for them." And then, from there: "What can I do, by myself or with others, to create a better situation?" And then, "What do I want to do differently, and how do I want to be different?" All these questions and all the possible alternatives are talked over and over between the social worker and his client, with the social worker always asking questions and making comments which will stimulate the client to understand and handle his feelings and to use the best powers of will, thought, and resources that he can muster to find his own answers. Of course, those "best powers" may fall short,

so the social worker contributes such knowledge or ideas as he may have for the client's consideration. Sometimes he takes such action or provides such means as the client does not have or cannot take alone.

In brief, the social worker helps his client continuously to weave to and fro between his feelings, his thinking, his behavior, his resources, and his goals. With people who are fairly well balanced and whose problems are not too stressful, this weaving together from problem recognition to problem solving is very quickly done. It did not take too long, for example, for the discussions to take place in the Norshore Philanthropic League which culminated in the decision to put all its energy and money into the project Tom Goodwin proposed. But when people are deeply troubled, when they are *"in* trouble," and their social situation is not very supportive, it may take a social worker many months of repeated talking together, feeling through, thinking through, trying out, before his client feels ready to try his own wings.

To try his own wings requires increased inner security and stability. But in many cases it also requires that there be tangible resources outside the person too. This means that

8. *The social worker must plan for, mobilize, and develop such opportunities and material means as are necessary for the solution of his client's problem; and show him how to avail himself of these resources.*

A caseworker like Mary Wright or Don Hart would find their ability to help people very narrow indeed if they could not reach out to resources present (some waiting to be tapped, some needing to be shaped to the client's special needs) in schools, clinics, relief agencies. A group worker like Judy Foster or Gabe Healy often needs the play materials and programs and play space that first draw their groups to the Neighborhood House. Community workers like Tom Goodwin and Gabe Healy (who, as you see, crosscut group work and community work) need constantly, as central to their building social services, to find and mobilize money, interest, man and womanpower and to suggest and shape the channels into which these resources should be poured.

The good social worker knows the organized resources in his community. He knows how essential they are to fill the lacks in people's lives. He may have to work for some time to get his particular client to want to use them. Sometimes he may have to bring the mountain to Mohammed and sometimes he may have to work with the resource (as Gabe Healy does with NOW) to get it to shape itself to the needs of a person or of the community. But he never loses sight of the fact that people live in relation to other people and to social conditions and institutions. The social worker is a bridging person, a linker between individuals and groups and the various opportunities and helps that our society has set up.

Beyond this every good social worker keeps his eyes and ears open to what services in his community are lacking, what unmet needs there are for which no resources exist, what kinds of concrete "helps" need to be developed. Caseworkers, particularly, are the advance scout people in this part of social work. Caseworkers deal with people in trouble. They know firsthand how frequently certain problems occur and what the needs seem to be. Their reports to supervisory and administrative personnel in their agencies about what people seem to be hurt by and to be wanting become the basis of planning by one or more agencies for change or new developments in social services.

There is one further aspect of what every social worker

does—or ought to do. That is to take some responsibility for social action.

"Social action" is a much-used and exciting phrase these days, but it is not always clear what people mean when they use it. Social work as an institution of our society is one form of social action. Within social work everything that is done— whether in the one-to-one encounters of the caseworker or the one-to-group encounters of the group worker or the group-to-group encounters of the community worker—is a form of social action. That is, they are all in the interest of changing or modifying in socially desirable directions the social-personal behavior of individuals and the structuring and functioning of their society. But in the special sense of its present-day usage in social work "social action" refers chiefly to the latter aspect, to the actions that shape or modify the policies and programs that affect large sectors of the population, "society."

If you listen to social workers today you may find that some of them have taken an either-or position on social action. Out of burning impatience for social reforms some social workers have pushed aside the kinds of social work help that are necessary to meet people's problems, as though this were unimportant, and they have said (or implied) that only radical reforms ought to be social work's present business. Radical reforms in many areas of our social life are essential. Many of them are presently under way. But until they are achieved— and until they are appraised in their actual consequences for people (for example, the building of public housing turns out to have brought many new social problems into being: many such projects have been concentrations of the chronically poor!)—until such reforms are accomplished, people—Mrs. Brown and Josie Green and the Blue Bloods, and the mothers who want a child care center—can't just sit and wait. They need and want the individual and immediate kinds of help which present social agencies provide. In short, *both* present-day social services and social action for better systems are essential. And every social worker ought to recognize this ongoing two-pronged nature of social welfare.

Social action for the everyday social worker usually takes place through his membership in and affiliation with his professional organization. (As a citizen—and his social work knowledge and firsthand firing-line experience should make him a particularly well-informed citizen—he may, of course, affiliate with all sorts of permanent or temporary groups and organizations devoted to issues of civil rights, civil liberties, neighborhood improvements, housing legislation, medical insurance and so on. The kinds and numbers of citizen social action groups are legion.)

Two major social-action routes are open to the social worker as a *professional* beyond his usual activity within the boundaries of his job. One is through his activity as a member of one of the social action committees of the National Association of Social Workers. These committees operate on a local and national basis. The other is as a supporter of the growing number of national social welfare organizations which are increasingly taking positions on and exerting influence in relation to social changes.

Through its committees on social policy and action the National Association of Social Workers has developed statements on public social policy and goals and has had continuous interchange with chapter committees working on selected social issues. Chapter committees have gathered data for legislative testimony and political pressure, have allied themselves with other groups and committees in the community in the interests of social policy or program reforms or innovations. Individual social workers may join these committees or may in various ways support their work.

Increasingly certain national social welfare organizations are turning their moneys, personnel, and influence resources to social action toward social welfare. The National Federation of Settlements and Welfare Centers, the Family Service Association of America, the National Jewish Welfare Board, and many others are allying themselves with progressive social action positions and pressures.

Off in the small orbit of his small job the individual social worker may sometimes feel himself to be a very small cog in the social-political wheels of social reform. Yet if he remains constantly alert, in every single case (whether that "case" is of a person or a group or a committee), to the idea that the test of social policy is the welfare of the individual man, he is the tester of social policies and programs and the witness to whether or not they work "in real life." His testimony, whether to his agency, to his professional organization, or to the social action groups he is attached to as a citizen should be loud and clear and soundly supported by his knowledge and firsthand experience.

What a social worker does is shaped in many important ways by what he is hired to do. What he is hired to do, in turn, is to carry out some part of some social agency or organization's purpose. So you need to know something about the kinds of places or organizations that will hire you if you become a social worker. That's what the next chapter is about.

four: *Where do social workers work?*

If you were to become a social worker, where you would work would depend, first of all, on what kind of social work you decided you wanted to do: whether you chose to be a caseworker, a group worker, or a community worker, or, as seems increasingly to be called for, some combination of two of these. Once you had made that choice, you'd have further choice ahead of you. Geographically your "where" could be almost anywhere in the country. But more important would be what sort of social problem you were interested in working with. Social agencies are set up to deal with special aspects of people's social needs. Where you would work would depend on your particular interest in particular problems as well as your particular capacities and training.

As you read what follows, remember this: Once you have mastered one of the major methods in social work, it is possible for you to work in many different social agencies or social work departments that use your particular method. For example, once you have become a caseworker you may work for

several years in a family service agency, then you may move
to a psychiatric clinic, then you may move from there (not too
frequent moves, hopefully!) to a child-treatment institution,
and so forth. Once you have become a group worker you may
work in a settlement house, you may take your next job in a
psychiatric hospital, and so forth. Social workers are a mobile
group—partly because so many new opportunities and challenges are opening up to them these days. And they are
increasingly versatile (depending in part on their training, of
course) in turning at times from their major practice method
to the use of one or both of the other helping methods. Thus
caseworkers who once only interviewed people one-to-one
are increasingly using group interviews, especially in family
problem cases; group workers and community workers find
the need for skilled individual interviews many times in their
work; indeed the lines between casework and group work
and between group work and community work are crossed
over many times by the present-day social work practitioner.
(If you'll look back at Chapter One you'll see illustrations of
this.)

Wherever you choose to work you will be the employee of
some established social agency or of the social service department of some other human welfare agency or social welfare
enterprise. (There is a small sector of highly experienced
social workers—both caseworkers and group workers—who
are self-employed, private practitioners; they will be discussed later.) Social agencies or social service departments or
the host of new special projects in social welfare that have
arisen in the past few years all carve out certain kinds of
human problems and needs on which they aim to specialize
or concentrate. No one of them can be all things to all men
and do so competently. Each agency arises in response to

certain recognized lacks or needs in people's lives. So *where* you would choose to work would be affected not just by geographical considerations but also by what aspect of human life problems you're most interested in.

A social agency is simply the formal organization of resources—money, services, and manpower—to meet certain kinds of social problems and to provide for certain social needs. It comes into being when citizens of a local community or of a nation recognize social needs for which dependable, organized, expert resources are necessary. Then an agency is created to perform special functions, to give help or offer opportunities. It may be supported by taxes, as are public assistance agencies, veterans' hospitals and clinics, community mental health clinics, court probation departments, etc. Or it may be supported by voluntary contributions, as are many of the family and child welfare agencies and clinics that you are accustomed to thinking of as "Red Feather," or Community Chest, agencies.

Every social agency must have a permit or a charter from official sources that says it meets certain standards. Every agency has a board of directors, or some similar governing body, that carries over-all responsibilities for the agency's activities. Every agency has rules and regulations that state its program, who is eligible for its services, how it aims to give those services. Its administrative and supervisory personnel —social workers—are accountable for its effective and efficient operation; and its practitioners—the social workers who actually *are* the agency in action—are you and your colleagues. You have direct contact with the people who look to the agency for the kinds of knowledge and services it holds and transmits through you.

Let's look first at the agencies longest established and longest part of the firm network of social service organizations.

Family Welfare Agencies

The family is the basic and most vital social unit in our society. So it is no wonder that the family welfare agency was one of the first kinds of social service agency to be developed, and that it remains the most central agency in the galaxy of social services.

A family's welfare depends first and foremost on having its food and shelter and basic clothing needs met. So the basic family welfare agencies are the tax-supported public assistance agencies which provide "relief," or money grants, to families (and individuals without families) for their basic health and decency needs. There are many reasons why people need relief. There are families of mothers and their children where the natural breadwinner, the father, is physically or mentally sick—sometimes temporarily, sometimes forever; where the father died or has deserted; where there never was a father—that is, where the children are the often pathetic result of sex relations outside of marriage; where the man who is father and husband has never adequately carried his responsibility; where the father has a job and works as hard as he can, but because he has no special skills or occupational preparation he is the last to be hired, the first to be fired, and even when he has work he earns too little to put milk in the children's stomachs and shoes on their feet.

Even if you go no further than this in thinking about families on relief you can see why there must be dependable organized means to provide money assistance. Perhaps you can also see why social workers rather than just money-hand-out machines are vitally necessary. It is because people—

men, women, and children—are all involved in these problems that make relief necessary. They are not just bodies, not just statistics. They *feel* these needs. Not only their stomachs are involved but also their sense of hope or despair, of being worthless or worthwhile, of being outcasts or accepted. Moreover, their problems are all different from one another. The family whose father lies bedridden has many quite different problems from the family where there never was a father, and both are different from the family where the husband and father is up against continuous unemployment. All these families, to be sure, have the problem of no money, but the reason for no money is different for each of them, as are the family strengths and difficulties and the possible solutions.

Family welfare begins with firm floor boards of economic security under a family's feet. But economic security does not guarantee personal and interpersonal contentment. Family troubles occur in every segment of society, among the rich as well as the poor. Quarrels and incompatibility between husbands and wives affect not only their own mental health but that of their children. Marital problems quickly give rise to parent-child problems, child-school problems, and husband-employment problems. And chain reaction may run in reverse: A child with physical or emotional problems may set off a whole chain of disruptions in the family life, affecting sisters and brothers, parents, neighboring children. Family unity may be split by troubled parent-child relationships. Parents and adolescent children may be locked in conflicts that undermine total family life. Aged parents may become saddening and heavy burdens for their adult children. And so on.

It was when communities recognized and became concerned about the emotional well-being of families as well as their economic welfare that family service agencies spread across the country. Today there are well over three hundred family service agencies in this country, supported by voluntary contributions (through Community Chests and federated funds), to provide counsel and help to husbands and wives, parents and young children, adult children and aged parents, who are caught up in conflicts that shake family or individual stability.

The voluntarily supported, so-called "private," family welfare agency today has another major function. Not only does it deal with all the emotional-social problems that rock family life and undermine the social functioning and personality development of its members; it is, in addition, an experimental laboratory where new approaches to family problems are being tried out. For example, family agencies have been experimenting with "family life education," where mothers and fathers meet in group sessions to learn more about child rearing and to anticipate and thus to avoid problems.

More recently a number of private agencies have been experimenting with "reaching out to the hard-to-reach." That is, there has been a fresh recognition that many people, particularly those who have been long deprived and downtrodden, fear or do not trust any agency representing "the establishment" and many other needful people do not even know of the existence of agencies that can help with their interpersonal problems. Thus family agency workers, on learning from teachers or neighbors or clergymen of families disrupted and disorganized by stress and vicissitudes, are in many instances going out to knock on doors to try to help such families to want social service help. It's a long, hard haul sometimes to continue to "reach out" in the face of suspicion or resistance or dead apathy. But because it is often the most hurt and needful people who have developed these attitudes (and for understandable reasons, surely) many family agencies and their social workers have set themselves the special task of trying to engage the socially alienated family in using the family welfare aid the community is ready to provide.

The social workers hired by family agencies are usually caseworkers. Each family—or one or two persons in it—is a "case," dealt with individually or in the family group. Most family service agencies, those that deal with problems of personal and interpersonal conflicts, employ only social workers with full professional education and training. The psychosocial problems they aim to ameliorate or resolve demand all the social and psychological knowledge and all the skills of social work—and then some!

There is, however, growing interest in these agencies in identifying whether there may not be some services that can be carried by volunteers or paraprofessionals. For example, aged people are often hungry for visitors, for someone who will listen to their complaints and reminiscences, who will bring some warmth and company and freshness into their often empty, drab lives. Social work aides could do this job well. Reach-out projects need and could use only partly trained personnel to win the trust and interest of people who feel too wide a social distance between them and the agency. A number of family agencies, formerly interested only in highly skilled professional staffs, are considering where and how to use paraprofessionals in a supplementary way.

In the public assistance agencies, so-called "relief" agencies, social workers with only B.A. degrees or lesser education are employed. The programs of Aid to Families of Dependent Children (AFDC), of Aid to the Blind, Old Age Assistance, Aid to the Permanently and Totally Disabled, and General Assistance (a kind of catchall for people in need who do not qualify under one of the other categories) are so massive, covering so many millions of men, women, and children, that the need for social workers is insatiable. Unhappily there is high turnover of social worker staffs in these agencies. Their need for interested, dedicated, compassionate social workers is paramount.

No one realizes this more than the supervisors and administrators of the public assistance agencies. Therefore there continue to be many efforts to give on-the-job training courses to workers who may have had little in their educational backgrounds to prepare them to understand people and the reasons for their behavior and needs. Moreover, there are strong encouragements (and scholarships) to caseworkers who qualify to go on to graduate schools of social work for full professional training. The concern of both federal and state governments to get competent and steady staffing for these massive programs of individual and family welfare is expressed also in the recent Congressional funding to develop undergraduate college courses in social welfare.

So, if you want to be a social worker but are not able (yet) to go on for professional training or not sure about whether it is for you or you for it, you may try yourself out in public assistance family welfare, particularly in the AFDC program for fatherless families, where harassed mothers and children hanging on to life by the skin of their teeth need all the resources and caring and family guidance they can get.

Child Welfare Agencies

Sometimes family life is already so torn to pieces, so sick, or so fragile by the time it comes to the attention of social workers that the children of the family are in danger of being —or already have been—seriously harmed. This harm to children may be actually physical, the result of brutal treatment or consistent neglect. Or the harm may be psychological. This almost always accompanies physical deprivation or hurt but may occur when the child is clean and well-fed too. For example, it occurs when the parent is indifferent, totally absorbed in himself and his own problems, when the parent is rejecting and harsh, or when, as is so often the case, the parent himself is only a child in an adult body, lacking the mental and emotional ability to be a real parent.

It was to protect the physical and personality development of children that child welfare agencies came into being. These are of many kinds. The federal government, through the Children's Bureau, and individual state departments of public welfare have developed a large network of public child welfare services. Along with these are many local child welfare agencies supported by community funds and sectarian groups. As you can understand, there is no group in our population to which people's hearts go out so readily or for whom people's purses open so widely as to helpless—and always hopeful—children.

The major kinds of child welfare service are these:

Under state auspices a great deal of work is done by caseworkers with parents and children in their own homes. There is considerable overlap here with family welfare work, of course, but usually the child welfare worker is called in when one or more of the children in a family is actually being badly neglected or mistreated. In these instances the caseworker tries to help the parents (or parent) work out such physical, economic, or emotional problems as undermine their ability to give their children the care and protection that they need.

When this doesn't work, when the parents are clearly unable to give decent care, the children may be taken from them for placement. Sometimes parents give them up voluntarily, even indifferently. Every day's city newspaper carries a story of parental neglect of children: the mother who has abandoned her infant; the parents who are trying to sell one of their children; the mother who frequents taverns for companionship and "blot-out" while her six-year-old "takes care" of the three younger children. Social workers understand the deep psychological sickness that makes for many of these situations, and when that sickness seems incurable children may be put in placement for many years—sometimes till they grow up. In some cases they may be surrendered by their parents for adoption. In some they may be placed in foster homes where healthy and fond foster parents may begin to heal their psychological wounds. Sometimes these children are placed in institutions.

The day of the large institution where children were regimented and massed like little prisoners is, happily, on the wane—not waning fast enough, to be sure, but many and fine institutions are being developed where children are given individual attention, sensitive treatment, schooling, and recreational advantages. Social workers are the chief planners and workers in these modern child-treatment institutions.

There are also those child-placement situations where parents deeply love and care for their children but must turn to the child welfare agency for placement because sickness, usually mental, makes it impossible to give parental care or because the child himself is too seriously disturbed to be able to live at home. Here, too, depending on the child's needs and resources, foster homes or institutions are used.

In all child welfare agencies caseworkers have at least three areas of operation. They work with the children themselves, helping them to understand and to bear the separation from their own homes and to make the best possible adjustment to their new environments. They work with foster parents and housemothers and housefathers, helping them to understand and deal with the many emotional problems most of these children bring with them. They work with the child's own parents, toward helping them to release the child from unhappy bondage or toward becoming better parents so that eventually they may reclaim their child.

Increasingly child welfare institutions are using group workers as part of their treatment programs. Sometimes the group workers are recreation directors, but often today they work with those children whose life experiences have made them afraid of or hostile toward others, and help them learn to work or play in a group and to relate to other children and adults in reasonably appropriate ways.

The problems of childhood and adolescence seem to be growing in number and complexity. Or perhaps it is that people are more keenly aware than ever before that "as the twig is bent, so grows the tree" and "the child is father to the man." In any case the demand for trained caseworkers and group workers to deal with frightened and anxious or chronically angry and delinquent children is a continuous and growing one. Along with the demand for more social workers in this field is the demand for more knowledge and quicker, better means of treatment of the many variations of parent-child problems that social workers see today. In child welfare as in family welfare there are many kinds of research and experimental efforts in progress.

In many communities family and child welfare agencies have come together and operate as one agency. You can see why. It is very difficult indeed to determine when a family-centered problem becomes a child-centered one.

Alongside these mergers is the development of many specialized family and child welfare agencies. For example, in more than one community you will find an agency specializing in problems of adolescents. In some you will find a nursery school set up for problem children, where teachers and family caseworkers work closely together. Another agency specializes in helping unmarried pregnant girls and women, providing the shelter and medical attention they need, counseling with them on whether to keep or give up their babies, finding and selecting prospective adoptive parents. A project in yet another agency focuses on finding people who would become good adoptive parents for children who have physical handicaps or who are of mixed racial backgrounds. Some family and some children's agencies are concentrating treatment and study efforts today on problems of young delinquents, and so forth.

You can see why most child welfare agencies would prefer to employ professionally trained social workers. Each child is such a complex little creature, growing as he breathes, sensitive and vulnerable to every physical, psychosocial stimulus that impinges on him, susceptible to quick and deep hurt or to quick and deep pleasure. How he develops, what his major life tasks are at various life stages, what makes for his emotional and physical health and what for its dwarfing or distortion—all these are part of what social work knowledge conveys. Add to this the complications in his parents themselves and within their open and subtle interrelationships, and to this add the crises and pressures that may occur in the child's social environment, and you get some notion of how wise and disciplined and knowledgeable a child welfare caseworker (or group worker) ought to be.

Nevertheless, many of the needs of growing children can be met by substitute "mothering" and supplementary helps in learning, whether that learning is how to spell or how to relate trustingly to another person. So there is room to be made in child welfare agencies, both public and private, for social work aides and paraprofessionals. One would hope that they would have had some undergraduate course work in child development and child psychology and/or on-the-job guidance and training in the particular needs of children in the particular problem situation to which the agency attends. But for people who love and respect children there is a widening margin for volunteer and paid social work aide jobs.

Socialization Agencies

Actually all social agencies could be designated by this name "socialization." I use it here instead of what used to be called "recreational agencies" or "leisure-time agencies." They are still called these in many places, but I am taking the liberty of renaming them because the fact is that when they are under social work auspices the aim of such agencies is to expand and enrich people's chances to engage themselves with other people in groups gratifyingly and in ways that develop their interpersonal competence and/or to engage themselves with such objects or tasks as "re-create" them personally.

Family and child welfare agencies are primarily to meet

already present problems that are so pressing and acute that
they cry out for help. But there are also social agencies that
are set up to *prevent* occurrence of need, that offer opportunities for recreation and association with other people and
for self-expression—agencies that may be said to be enrich-
ers of people's environments. These are largely group work
agencies—boys' clubs, neighborhood and settlement houses,
"Y's," camps, community centers. Chiefly they use group
workers to provide the means by which people—adults as
well as children—might re-create their workaday selves,
stretch their horizons, facilitate wholesome association with
others. These agencies, when they are manned by professionally trained social group workers, offer not only the *place*
where people can get together and the *materials* and *activities* that people can get involved in, but also the *leadership*
that keeps in the forefront the idea that group activity is for
the development of good communication and cooperation
among the group members. The group worker's objective is
that what is learned at the agency may be carried into living
on the outside—into family relationships, work relationships,
everyday neighbor and social relationships.

To the casual eye—and often to the user himself—a settlement or "neighborhood house" or "community center" may
seem just a place where adults or children may drop in to "fill
in time" or "do something interesting." These are certainly
acceptable reasons for the existence of places that provide
constructive means by which these motives can be satisfied.

More and more, however, professional social workers have
been concerned with the loss of natural neighborliness especially in urban life, with the loss of natural easy means of
connection between people with like interests, with, in short,
the need to provide some "centering" in people's lives. Add

to this the desirability that such centering should produce two further results: one, increased competence to manage oneself effectively in relationships with other people, and, two, increased practice in decision making and problem solving together with others. Both are central to a good society. So it is that the group workers who are the lead social workers in these kinds of agencies are concerned that people should find "fun" and "interest" and "re-creation" in ways that build into their social competence.

Since their beginning group work agencies (as these socialization agencies are called when they are referred to by the major method they use) have used volunteers as leaders of some of their groups. Especially was this true when groups were formed around some special interest area—a baseball team, art work, camera clubs. Professionally trained group workers have been the supervisors and in-service trainers of such volunteers. Today many such neighborhood centers are housing groups whose purpose and actions are supported by special poverty-war funds for educational and employment training, for instance, for group organizations to develop "grass roots" resources and facilities. Trained group workers and community workers are sometimes the leaders and often the professional consultants to such groups. For leaders and aides to the continuity and directedness of such groups there promises to be a considerably expanded use of paid, partly trained social workers, trained within college or even junior college courses or on the job by professional group and community workers.

Councils of Social Agencies

As soon as a community sets up several kinds of social service and incorporates them into various agencies, the necessity for planning and clearing among those agencies becomes plain. It is evident, too, that there will be need for fund raising and fair apportionment of community moneys among the various agencies. Such apportionment ought to be decided by facts about what services are most needed, which overlap and can be dispensed with, what gaps need to be filled, and so on. In short, community planning and action require the development of welfare councils, community chests and councils, councils of social agencies—all of them for the purpose of planning, organizing, and supporting the social services.

Much of the work of improving the social services, of calling attention to unmet needs, comes from study done by social work researchers. The problems have been placed before them by the various agencies whose caseworkers and group workers have their fingers on the pulse of the people in the community. The front-line reports and suggestions of caseworkers and group workers are usually relayed through their agency's executives and directors to council committees for consideration and planning. Study of problems or needs results in appropriate action by community workers and their committees.

Actually, a council of social agencies or a community fund agency is not a direct service agency. It is rather a fund-raising, planning, and coordinating body, made up of representatives of service agencies plus representatives of other groups in the community. As you saw when you visited Tom Goodwin, its social workers are fact finders, appraisers, and planners in relation to community needs and problems; they are fund raisers, interest raisers, persuaders, and coordinators of agency and citizen efforts to meet those problems.

Increasingly in these past few years there have arisen self-organized groups, usually formed around special community interests or problems that have operated outside the usual family of social agencies. They are often "indigenous" groups, made up of the persons within sectors of the community, both those whose own needs push them to action and those who add their effort to the push because of their belief in and conviction about the "cause." (Gabe Healy's Neighborhood Organization of Women—NOW—pressing and planning for a day care center was one such group.) Such groups often go to welfare councils for advice, funding, cooperation. The councils' professional community organization social workers or their research workers will act as their consultants or advocates or cooperators. Sometimes such newly formed "grass roots" or "indigenous" groups hire a professional community worker as part-time consultant or executive. (Only rarely can they afford his full-time services.) But they may also hire a community worker who, though he has only some theoretical background, has demonstrated his practical know-how and skill in administration or community organization. And sometimes, as with NOW, these organizations will tie up with already going organizations which, like the Neighborhood House, seek to promote community participation and self-help efforts.

Up to this point you have seen those agencies that are "primary social agencies." That is to say they are administered and manned by social workers. They may use members of other professions—medicine, law, education, etc.—as consultants and aides, but their core purpose is "social service," and they are staffed by social workers.

But another large group of agencies hires social workers for their particular contributions of knowledge and their special competence. These are schools, child guidance clinics, medical and psychiatric clinics and hospitals, courts and correctional agencies, community mental health clinics, and a host of small, newly emerging organizations for community action on special problems.

You may wonder what social workers do in all these places —what they're wanted for. With all their differences you'll note that all these kinds of social institutions are human welfare agencies. A school to teach children the three R's, a hospital to mend broken bones, a juvenile court to mete out justice, all different, all have a common need for social workers. It is for these reasons:

1. Many times people cannot seem to use the opportunities that are open to them (such as education or medical care). Even when social opportunity is present and good it sometimes is feared or misunderstood by the person for whom it was set up. Thus a child may be afraid of school or a parent may feel helpless in the face of a big school system and thus feel unable to explain to the teacher or principal why she keeps her children out so often. An adult may have a generalized fear of hospitals, or resentments about the way he was treated when he last saw a doctor, or even some strong need to deny that he (or his children) ought to have medical care for some symptoms they're showing. So medical settings and schools look to their social workers to be the interpreters, explainers, and linkers between people who need a service but for some reason in themselves cannot seem to use it.

2. There may be reasons in the "setting" itself that make

it fearsome or difficult for a person to connect with it. Impatient personnel, or inadequate understanding on their parts, or rules that ought to be bent or even broken to suit individual needs—these obstacles to the use of service are often ascertained and appraised by the social worker. The social worker then becomes the interpreter and explainer of the *person* to the *place* (to the teacher, the doctor) and often, in addition, a persuader in the modification of some part of the agency system in order that it will seem hospitable to the needing person.

3. There may be conditions in the person's life situation that call for social work aids of a material as well as psychological nature, that affect how well the person uses and benefits by the services that are available to him. At the simplest level: a mother whose child does not have whole shoes cannot send him off to school on a snowy day. The school social worker knows at once where and how to connect with the relief agency to get some action going on shoes. At a more complex level: a mentally ill but recovering patient who is about to be released from the psychiatric hospital on a "trial visit" home cannot just be ushered out to make it on his own. To prevent another breakdown and to promote a reasonably good experience the psychiatric social worker will work in a two-pronged direction: to prepare the patient for what he might experience on the outside, and how he may deal with it, and to lay a careful groundwork of anticipation and planning with the patient's family which often fears or resents the patient's homecoming, or, even if they want it, do not know how to deal with him helpfully.

In short, the use of social service in those human welfare institutions that offer legal, medical, religious, psychiatric, educational services is toward facilitating the linkage and connection between the person and the available services. It is toward making available such material means and psychological assistances and individualization as the person may need in order to benefit from those services.

Whenever people seem unable, because of factors within themselves or for any external reason, to use the educational, legal, medical, and psychiatric services they need, social caseworkers are called upon to help them overcome the emotional or social obstacles. Each of these places where social workers are part of a team with another profession deserves separate explanation.

Medical Social Work Departments

Hospitals of all kinds use social caseworkers as part of the medical teams in the treatment of the sick. The establishment of a medical social work department in a hospital means that the doctors have recognized that a patient is more than his sickness. It means that one or more of the doctors in authority have the conviction that "getting well" or adjusting to chronic illness or even just following the doctor's orders is greatly influenced by many factors in a patient's life.

One factor may be the patient's frame of mind, his feelings and attitudes about himself, his illness, the hospital, whatever. Another may be the patient's home situation—what's happening to his wife and children while he's in the hospital; or, if he's an outpatient, what circumstances at home—social, economic, interpersonal—underpin his recovery or undermine his strivings toward health. Being sick is sometimes a luxury. If wages are cut off or if medicines are costly, a patient may need help in making connections with social agencies that can provide assistance.

Then there are those situations in which the illness of one family member can undermine the social and psychological well-being of the whole family. When, for instance, a mother is hospitalized and leaves helpless and worried children at home, or when she is bedridden at home and there is no one to cook supper or wash underwear or to say, "Now it's bedtime," a family's stability is liable to be shaken. Often friends or relatives may come in to fill the gaps and pick up dropped roles. But many families have no "natural" helpers, and in these cases the medical social worker acts to find the resources in the community (such as homemaker services) or to offer family members such moral support and release from their fears that they remain steady in the face of trouble.

Hospital and clinic social caseworkers (called "medical social workers" in these particular settings) typically give these kinds of help: They obtain the material means that a patient and/or his family may need for social, economic, physical, or psychological well-being. They deal with the actions and attitudes of people whose behavior affects the patient's welfare. They work directly with the patient himself, helping him to talk about and get free of anxieties or confusions or misapprehensions about himself, his family, his future; helping him to consider ways and means of coping with his handicap (if he has one); making arrangements for him with convalescent homes or rehabilitation centers. And they work with doctors and other staff people, helping them to know the social and psychological factors that have important bearing on the patient's illness and recovery.

The "where" of medical social work is in hospitals, big or small, and in outpatient clinics. On any one day you will be at a patient's bedside on the ward as he tells you about the letter from his wife full of her worries about money and the children's behavior; you will be in a doctor's office, discussing with him some of the reasons this patient doesn't seem to want to get well; you may be visiting the patient's wife, trying to lead her to some understanding of her husband's need for her courage and moral support; you may, in short, be in all the places where there is need for the understanding and handling of the social and personal problems that sickness brings.

Medical social workers are usually professionally trained. But the need for paraprofessional personnel and social work aides is nowhere more urgent than in hospital settings. There are all kinds of possible and necessary services to the sick and near-sick to be selected from the trained medical social worker's job and then paid for. Bedside visiting and listening, group play with sick or convalescent children, psychological preparation of children (and adults too) for tests or medicines or surgery, helping people find their way through the bewildering mazes of hospital procedures, making arrangements for wheelchair or for toys or for a change of housing (so that the heart patient will no longer have to walk three flights of stairs to her apartment)—all these kinds of services make the difference between a patient who is sick and one who is also heartsick. And these can be given by paraprofessionals, especially if they are given on-the-job guidance by the professionally prepared medical social worker.

Psychiatric Hospitals and Clinics

In hospitals for the mentally ill, in the wards of general hospitals set aside for mentally and emotionally disturbed patients, in clinics to which disturbed or distressed people—young and old—come, social caseworkers are called (again named by their setting) "psychiatric social workers." In recent years, with a rapidly growing interest in dealing with patients in groups as well as singly, psychiatric hospitals and clinics have begun to draw social group workers too.

In mental and emotional, as in physical, illness patients have to be helped to work at getting well, and whether they are ready and able to work at it is heavily influenced by the people to whom they are emotionally tied (their parents, spouses, children) and also by whether the life situation they have to cope with is too full of difficulty or is manageable.

The psychiatric social worker, like his medical counterpart, is deeply involved in helping the patient himself and other people (members of his family usually) to cope with the difficulties in the environment that make living hard to handle or to face. These difficulties may be obvious, like too hard a job with too little gratification, or they may be subtle ones, like the interplay of feelings and attitudes between the patient and his intimates, feelings that create or feed his illness. Wives, husbands, parents, children, all of us really, find it difficult to understand another person's emotional disturbance. Even when we understand it, it is extremely hard to live with and to bear. The moody or unreasonably hostile or frankly crazy behavior rouses all sorts of miserable feelings, not only in the mentally disturbed person himself but also in those close to him. Anger, resentment, guilt, anguish—all these and other emotions complicate an already unhappy situation. For the patient and his family, life becomes full of problems, hazards, and fears. Here are just a few expressions of them:

"How *can* I put my wife into an institution? She'll be so terribly unhappy there!"

"Yes, it's true that my son has shut himself up in his room for weeks and won't see anyone. But don't you think he's just

—well, moody? I mean, no one in our family has ever had a mental breakdown!"

"It's impossible to keep this man at home! He goes into such terrible rages and threatens us and talks to himself, and the children and I are afraid for our lives."

"I know I should try—I know I should try to be interested —but everything inside of me says, 'Die, die, die.' "

"But we have no room in the house to take Father back! We moved into a smaller place when he went into the hospital four years ago—and now there's no place for him. Besides— he's still really not altogether 'there,' you know."

"Sure, I love him. But how long can a woman wait for a man to get well?"

"I don't know if I can get a job or not any more. I don't know if anyone wants me. I'm sort of scared to go out of here."

You can see what the psychiatric social worker is faced with and what he may have to do. Like the medical social worker, he deals continuously with the people whose lives are bound up with the patient, whose attitudes and actions affect those of the patient. Like the medical social worker, he gets the facts about the patient's social, economic, psychological circumstances which help to explain the nature of the illness or disturbance, and which may need to be taken into account in treatment. Like the medical social worker, he may work directly with the patient (in careful consultation with a psychiatrist), hearing out his problems, providing a warm and supporting safety island of relationship. He guides, leading the patient in small steps, often over long weeks of many interviews, to see more clearly, to feel more sure, and to cope with people and conditions outside himself.

The group worker in the psychiatric hospital or clinic

works with several patients at a time, trying to get them to relate to him and to one another. Getting well and being well are largely made up of being unafraid of oneself and unafraid in relationships with other people.

Both psychiatric caseworkers and psychiatric group workers operate in a team relationship with one or more psychiatrists (heads of the team) and psychologists in clinical settings. In hospitals they work with many other professional people too—nurses, occupational therapists, pharmacologists; the list is a long one. Today's psychiatric treatment centers are complex places because mental illness and emotional disturbance are complex conditions. The social worker is only one of the many professional persons bending their efforts to understand and deal with the mysteries of man's psychological health and sickness.

As in general medical hospitals and clinics, there is a rapidly increasing interest in psychiatric settings in the use of partially trained personnel to supplement the work of professional social workers and to take over some of the jobs that have fallen to the latter simply because they needed to be done and there was no one else to do them. Many young college students have taken summer jobs or done volunteer work as "psychiatric aides" in mental hospitals. Their interest and patience and tender loving care have been deeply moving to many patients who, before, had felt abandoned, uncared for, isolated from the world. So the possible uses of such paid social service aides with only some undergraduate training are viewed with growing optimistic conviction by psychiatric hospital administrations.

Community Mental Health Centers

Almost a revolution in the view and treatment of mental illness has occurred in the past ten years. One of its major thrusts has been to bring the hospitalized, mentally ill patient out from the isolated, "sick" world of the hospital and into the community where, within the limits of his illness or disturbance, he can take part in normal social life. Sparked by the recommendation of the Joint Commission on Mental Illness and Health and supported by federal and state funding, a vast network of "comprehensive community mental health services" is spreading across the country, concentrated usually in urban centers. The idea is to prevent hospitalization of mentally and emotionally disturbed people, when possible, to provide such treatment as will make it possible for people with psychological problems to continue to carry as many of their normal life roles as possible (as worker, as student, as parent), and to so affect the social environment as to make it "health inducing" rather than undermining.

That is a tremendously ambitious program, and it is no wonder that in many places it falls far short of its aim. But its aim is a vital one and many kinds of community health workers—psychiatrists, psychologists, and great numbers of social workers and social work aides—are pouring their energies into trying to make it work.

You can see why such a widespread effort to keep people functioning in their social relationships and to "socialize" their environment so that it is conducive to their well-being should call for social workers in large numbers. You can also see how paraprofessional or social work aides, especially those who are themselves close by class or color or life experience to troubled and disadvantaged people, would be tremendously useful in connecting people with sources of help, in finding jobs, in finding and linking people up with leisure-time opportunities, in finding and arranging for decent housing, and so on. "Comprehensive mental health service" means comprehensive coverage of all aspects of people's lives that can either undermine or build up their mental health. Caseworkers, group workers, and community workers are all essential to the planning and delivery of the wide range of services called for. The use of aides and paraprofessional social workers is growing and is recognized for its potential and proved values.

Child Guidance Clinics

The child guidance. clinic specializes in the problems of young children. These clinics are set up sometimes as separate agencies and sometimes as part of general or pediatric hospitals.

Sometimes it is hard to say how the work of a child guidance clinic is different from a child or a family welfare agency. In any of these the caseworker may deal primarily with the parents or primarily with the child. In the child guidance clinic the psychiatrist is the basic treatment authority. Family and child welfare agencies that work with disturbed children always have psychiatrists as consultants to their casework staffs. Thus, whether in a family agency, a child welfare agency, or a child guidance clinic, when a young child shows serious emotional or mental disturbance both a social caseworker and a psychiatrist are usually involved. Their division of labor—who takes on the treatment of the child and who takes on that of the mother or mother and father—is worked out differently at different times and places and in relation to the case needs.

On one thing there is full agreement: For reasons that are not entirely clear, the children coming to child welfare agencies and guidance clinics today seem far more disturbed than were the children of an earlier generation. Far more needs to be understood about the causes of their emotional disturbance in order that better treatment may be worked out. In this effort social workers, psychologists, psychiatrists, and others agree that all kinds of study, fresh ideas, and combinations of professional effort are needed. Child guidance, which has such a pleasant and friendly sound, has become one of the most puzzling areas of need in both social work and psychiatry, and social workers are involved in it in almost any setting in which they work.

School Social Work

Just as the medical social worker came into being when medicine discovered the "whole man," so school social work began when educators discovered the "whole child." It started when some teachers were concerned enough to make visits to the homes of children who were having troubles in the classroom or whose appearance and behavior indicated that something was probably wrong. The usefulness of visiting teachers led to their development as one part of the school's responsibility to children. Most of the early visiting teachers lacked knowledge and understanding of the social-psychological problems of children; their training was largely, of course, in understanding children who came to learn and who were for the most part able to do so. Even those visiting teachers who deeply understood children lacked the background for dealing with the family needs and situations which were so often at the bottom of the child's difficulty. More and more, social work training began to be called for. School social workers are the trained caseworkers who are adjuncts and aids to a modern school's educational program.

School social workers work with children who are referred by teachers for a variety of reasons. The problems run all the way from "no shoes," "no breakfast," "family life is completely disorganized" to problems of emotional difficulties that are interfering with the child's learning or normal development. "Michael is a very withdrawn little boy—seems to be isolated from other children and to be living in a dream world," says one teacher. From another: "Fred is a potential delinquent—always fighting, always a chip on his shoulder—cheats without batting an eyelash. Yet his psychological tests show a very high IQ." From another: "Betsy is continually absent. Says her mother is sick and cries all the time, and she, Betsy, must stay home and care for the younger children."

As you can see, every one of these referrals calls for someone to get the facts about the child, his family situation, and the reasons for the problem, and then to work out some plan for tackling the problem. The school social worker gathers this data, but because he usually covers a large school or even a number of large schools he cannot be the caseworker on all the situations referred to him. He does some preliminary interviewing with teacher, child, parents—sometimes one, sometimes all—and then mobilizes other resources for cases that need intensive work. He acts as a link between school, child, family, and the welfare agencies, the relief agencies, the clinics, or whatever other social services seem to have relation to the problem.

On less serious problems the school social worker may

work with a boy or girl in the school office, talking over his problems, helping him to "get on the ball" again. He may also see parents in a guiding-advisory way over several interviews. He does a good deal of discussion with the teachers themselves, helping them to get perspective on some of their problem students and to cope with this or that bit of problem behavior. You may remember that Don Hart, a family caseworker, led a discussion group for teachers in one of the city schools. Had there been a school social worker in that school (or in the school system) such discussion with the teachers would probably have been carried by her.

Not all school systems use social workers. Many boards of education believe they cannot afford them or do not see their use. (You remember that Tom Goodwin, community worker, had as one of his major developing projects that of getting the school system in his city to install a social work department.) As education increasingly recognizes the relationship between learning problems and problems inside the child or in his home situation, the need for school social workers as links between school and home and between school learning and emotional stability is increasingly being recognized.

Mostly school social workers are caseworkers. Sometimes group methods are used, however, as when groups of children with like problems are dealt with in group discussions or when teachers are seen. The requirement for a school social worker is for advanced professional education. The complex of school-home-child-teacher-parents that must always be dealt with takes considerable knowledge of their dynamics and considerable skill in their management.

Courts and Correctional Institutions

There was a time when courts meted out justice and its consequent rewards and punishments to all who came before them. Then came a day when it was recognized that reward and punishment decisions, if they were to be truly just, had to take into account both the circumstances and the conditions that led to the problem and the consequences that would result from the judicial decisions. This was particularly apparent in cases involving child offenders, young delinquents, and parental neglect. Lawyers and social workers and prominent laymen brought about court reforms early in this century. Family courts and juvenile courts were established for cases that were heavily weighted with social and psychological problems, where rehabilitation seemed possible. In some places—unfortunately as yet in a minority of places—courts dealing with cases of families and children have taken social caseworkers onto their staffs. Their jobs: to get the facts about the problems and the people involved in the cases and to make recommendations to the judge about what ought to be done. ("This family seems able and willing to stay together provided supervision can be got from the Children's Agency. . . ." "This boy has been so long and consistently mistreated by his stepfather, and the latter seems himself to be so delinquent, that we recommend his removal from the home to an institution.") Often, beyond this, their jobs are to follow up on family neglect and delinquency cases and to get the services for them that will better the situation.

There was a time when probation—putting a person on a test of good behavior—and parole—putting a person who has been imprisoned on trial freedom—were simply checkup, report-in systems. Today both probation and parole officers are increasingly seen as rehabilitation workers. In enlightened court systems they are seen as representing the court's benign arm and its helping hand. To the offender they say in effect, "I'm here to be of help to you. I'm here as the court's attempt to guard against repeating your mistakes—and more than that, to help you find outlets and aims that are satisfying to you *and* to our society." You can see why social workers —or men and women with at least partial training in social casework—began to be wanted as probation and parole officers.

There was a time when young delinquents were sent to reform schools which were so poorly set up and so poorly staffed that they were scarcely schools at all, and any reforming that took place was often in the wrong direction. That time, sad to say, is still here. Most reformatories in most states are still barracks where boys, and sometimes girls, "do time." Yet here and there are glimmers of light and change, enough to make one hopeful that with time and effort and money the institutions that harbor delinquents can really become schools, learning places that reform or refashion the motivations and behavior patterns of the young people in them. In those model correctional institutions, where the aim and the resources are to help young offenders become acceptable members of society, caseworkers and sometimes group workers operate as part of the correctional team.

In short, as court and correctional systems become more socialized, more humanized, their use of social workers as part of their rehabilitation programs increases. But it is happening very slowly. Moreover, these are not easy places in which to work. The wheels of justice grind slowly, and sometimes to a caseworker eager for quick change they seem to grind in cumbersome and blind ways. The young people brought into court and their families often seem to be hard nuts to crack, and it takes deep understanding and patience to stand by until they are ready to trust you. The conditions of work are often rough. But being brought to court is a point of no return for many youngsters, unless someone stands ready at that point to help reverse the vicious circle they're so often caught up in. Slowly but increasingly social workers are being drawn in to help "correction" mean not punishment but opportunity.

Increasingly the professionally prepared social worker, whether caseworker or group worker, is being used as supervisor and as consultant to the large number of probation and parole officers who have no actual training in their career field. The need for men (mostly men are needed though there are many women law violators too and so there are also positions for women workers in this area) who are firm, strong, able to "take it," and who are understanding, compassionate, and able to "dish it out" (when necessary) is a very great need indeed. Here again there is some advantage in the probationer or parolee's feeling that the social worker he must "report to" or talk things over with is someone who talks his language and is able to put himself in his shoes (even though he may disapprove of those shoes!).

For many would-be social workers this "comes naturally." Such persons, with supervision or on-the-job courses on subjects such as the delinquent personality, the "culture of crime," the techniques of establishing a working relationship, and so forth, may do an excellent job with boys and men who up to this point have seen all authority as punitive only and are surprised sometimes to find that a respectable someone is *with* them, wanting to help them "make it straight."

Other Places Where Social Workers Work

So far you've been reading about the main "wheres" of social work's employment. But there are two other categories of "where." One is a group of social or other human welfare agencies that focuses on certain kinds of rather special problems. The other is a range of projects, agencies, organizations that have literally grown up like weeds in these past few years, all aiming to deal with some aspect of inner city problems—poverty, social discrimination, housing, jobs. Many of these employ at least one professional social worker for research or consultation or planning.

In the first group are those agencies that deal with certain unexpected crises in people's lives. Travelers Aid, for example, deals with people in transit who for reasons of mental or physical incapacity may be lost or confused or who for loss or lack of money may be stranded. Runaway children and young adolescents are frequent among the hungry, sleepless, and bedraggled travelers they help. Individual casework, understandably, is the method used by Travelers Aid. It uses many volunteers to man its desks in airports and bus and railroad stations, but its professional social workers are behind the scenes for help in complicated cases and for supervision of aides.

The American Red Cross is another agency that employs professionally trained social workers for family welfare services to men in the armed forces (and their families), to ex-servicemen (and their families), and in disasters that overwhelm communities (such as flooded areas).

The United States Army commissions social workers with graduate degrees to work as psychiatric and medical social work officers. In its general and neuropsychiatric hospitals, its disciplinary barracks, its reconditioning centers, in short for men who are in difficulty in coping with the demands of military life, the army wants qualified social workers to work in collaboration with its medical and psychiatric personnel.

Several national social agencies (The Florence Crittenton association and the Salvation Army are the major ones) devote themselves to work with women and girls who are pregnant out of wedlock, sheltering them in their pregnancy period, connecting them with necessary prenatal and hospital care, counseling them on all the emotional and practical problems and the conflicts that go along with having a baby without marriage. For this kind of guidance and counseling both training and maturity are desirable in the social worker. Caseworkers for the individual girls (and their families) are most frequently employed in these agencies, but group workers are increasingly being used in maternity homes, where many young women spend the months of their pregnancy, for purposes of group discussion of their common problems such as "Is it better to keep your baby or to give it in adoption?" and "What are some of the problems you'll have to deal with, whichever you choose?" or "How can you be a good mother if you haven't finished school, or got married, or had your own life satisfactions?"

The final grouping of organizations that employ social workers can scarcely be identified as a group. As has been indicated, they are newly formed projects, often with small or uncertain budgeting means, often pushing up from the grass roots (or should one say, more accurately, from the broken pavements?) to meet some pressing and recognized need. A number of such organizations and projects are supported by the Office of Economic Opportunity. Head Start is probably one that is best known. Under various names in different localities there are neighborhood development operations. There are urban affairs councils supported by combinations of government funds and contributions by businessmen, by churches, by private foundations. There are youth commissions to study and plan means to combat delinquency. Increasingly certain political offices (a mayor, a governor, a congressman) look to social workers to provide them with facts and perspectives on social problems and programs. The scatter and the opportunities are widespread and seem to be multiplying.

What do all these projects want from social workers? Many of them want the people who can carry decisions and plans into action, who can carry out "what ought to be." For this function it is possible to train and give direction to indigenous workers, neighborhood people themselves. To supplement their work and to provide a dependable core staff it is possible to use competent (and dedicated) young college and junior college graduates who have had some basic course work in sociology, social psychology, and social welfare.

What many of these organizations find they want and need in addition are social workers with training in research (to get and put together the facts of both need and resources), with knowledge of welfare policies and programs at every level of government, with ability to lay out blueprints, to consult with people, to motivate them in desired directions, to analyze the ways and means and the wheels within wheels by which people promote or block a project. Such social workers are usually professionally trained community workers. Even a project such as VISTA (Volunteers in Service to America) under the OEO has employed professional community workers to develop training programs and projects, to administer large programs, to write proposals for supporting grants, and so on.

As you can see, social workers work almost any "where," that is, anywhere that an organization or agency sees the promotion of human well-being as its major purpose. Often social work is the central profession, "in charge"; at other times it is a collaborating profession, in teamwork with others; at other times and in other places it provides consultation, information, coordinating, and linkage services.

Social workers are mostly salaried employees, hired for their competence and skill in carrying out an organization's purposes. However, there has developed over the past two decades a growing group of private practitioners in social work. At first these were caseworkers only, those who specialized in counseling and guidance of individuals able to pay fees for help with personal and interpersonal problems. More recently, as group therapies have come into prominence, a number of group workers have entered private practice.

After some years of heated professional debate about whether private practice is "social" (a question still not satisfactorily answered for many social workers) the National Association of Social Workers gave private practice its sanction. There are stipulations which standardize such practice: the practitioner must identify himself as a social worker, not a "psychotherapist" or "counselor"; he must have a master's degree; he must have had a certain number of years of competent and adequately supervised practice experience in recognized social agencies before he can qualify for private practice—and so on. The fact is that most social workers in private practice—there are several thousands of them at present—are also employees of social agencies. Their private practice is mostly part time. One of the reasons for this is the necessity they feel to keep close to professional concerns and commitments, and to benefit from the stimulation of coworkers and agency experimentations.

What all this says is that for a would-be social worker the question "Where shall I work?" leads to many answers. The choice may be limited at first, when you have but little experience or skill. But as your experience grows in depth and breadth and as you prove your competence, your choices and your chances will be over a wide and interesting range of places. And then the question becomes "How do I get there? How do I get to be a social worker?"

five: **How do you get to be
a social worker?**

Let's start with you, as a person. Then we'll go on to the kind
of education you'll need if you want to become a professional
social worker, to make it your career, and then the lesser
education you'll need if you want a job in social welfare but
as a partly professional social worker or as a social work aide.

To be a social worker requires that you be a certain kind
of person. Sometimes when some of us old hands begin to line
up specifications for the kind of person we want in the
profession we seem to be asking for saints, not human beings!
But the fact is that there are some qualities a social worker
just can't do without—and perhaps as they are set down here
you can do some self-analysis and ask yourself: Am I such a
person?

First, a social worker must be more "people oriented" than
"thing oriented." He must be concerned more with how people work than with how things work, and even when he
thinks about things it ought to be in relation to whether they
are good or bad for people. He must be more "action toward

change" oriented than content with the status quo. Beyond being interested in people he must have some fairly strong wish to help people struggle up and out of their problems into a better life.

An interest in people means more than liking people or liking to be with them. It means a lively curiosity about all the ways people are and act, about their kindliness, their brutality, their depravity, their courage, about their smiling, sorrowing, hating, loving—all the emotions of that mysterious thing called personality.

Along with this interest must go real feeling for people. You should find in yourself some leap-up of feeling with and for others, some sense that you are not only an observer of another person but a participator in his emotions. We call this empathy, which is to say that you spontaneously put yourself into the shoes of another and know what he feels. You may feel compassion for him if he is in trouble or you may feel at one with him in his happiness or triumph. There will, of course, always be some people you cannot identify with— someone who is cruel, a bully, a swindler—and social workers encounter such people too. Then the social worker's professional discipline reminds him to "hate the sin but not the sinner," and he gives himself over to trying to understand what makes for the distortions and ugliness in this human being.

It would be a poor social worker indeed who could see only goodness in people, who had to deny (because he could not bear) human frailty. Human beings, all of them, you and I and all the people who come to social work, are "bad" as well as "good." An old popular song went "There's a little bit of bad in every good little girl!" That little bit of bad may grow big and permeate the human being's total personality under some unhappy circumstances and experiences. Or it may be a very minor part of our makeup because we've been lucky enough to have life experiences that have, as we say, brought out the good in us. Anyway, this is why social work does not look for saints or Pollyannas as its practitioners (even if it could find them!). We hope you've got some "badness" in you. We hope you are aware of your badness, that is, that you recognize that right now, or at times in the past, you have had mean thoughts or wishes, maybe have done mean things, that you have felt hate, anger, envy—in short, that you have been a human being.

The point is that it is not possible to understand in another person what you have never known, at least in some small degree, in yourself. Therefore, a person must know himself in preparation for knowing others. The test of his ability to help others—to be a social worker—will be his capacity to recognize his own desires and urges and then to contain and control them in order to use himself in service to another. This capacity is part of maturity. In the education of a social worker, his capacity to feel with and for other people and to manage his own feelings will be tested over and over again, and will be strengthened.

Besides interest in the feeling for people and self-management ability, a social worker ought to have in him a quick sensitivity to justice and injustice, to right and wrong, to fair and unfair, especially as these values relate to the interaction between society and its members. You know this sensitivity in yourself when you see or hear of people being exploited, deprived, discriminated against, pushed under, and so on. Social conditions that cut off people's rights to decent living conditions and undermine their self-respect should bother you whether you actually see them or only read about them in the paper. A good social worker never loses this "divine discontent" or his sense of social justice.

Beyond this righteous indignation should be some sense that you want to do something about the situation. Doing something may involve others than yourself—but at least you want to put a hand to the task. Doing something that is appropriate and effective will be surer and better directed once you've had the social work education that helps you know more about your society and the social resources, programs, and policies that affect so many people's lives. A social work education will give direction to your "divine discontent," but the spark of it must be in you.

Then there's that basic, all-important quality we call maturity. Everyone talks about it—but hardly anyone can define it. Maturity, for any given age, means something like this: Basically and usually you feel fairly steady, fairly secure. You feel more at one with your world than at odds with it. You feel reasonably able to cope with your life tasks. When you are frustrated or depressed—as who isn't at times?—you are able to bear it in the expectation that you'll get on top of that problem too.

All of this, you'll note, is in relative terms, more rather than less, reasonably rather than ideally—because no one is totally mature all of the time. The point is that, as you have already seen, social work is a demanding profession. You will encounter in it problems that are shocking, harrowing, nagging, depressing. You will be working with people who are caught up in many conflicts and troubles and, therefore, emotions. And you must have built-in shock absorbers, which is what this elusive thing called maturity provides.

One part of these shock absorbers is humor. The trouble with humor is that you can't cultivate it: it's in you or it's not.

When you have it, it helps a lot. Many very funny things happen when you're working with people. But there are many frustrating things too; and it is for these latter that you will need the buoy of humor.

Patience and courage are important too (even if they sound like old-fashioned virtues). You need patience and persistence because people and circumstances simply will not change just because a social caseworker says, "Look, you ought to do this, not that," or because a community worker says, "Hey! I've got a blueprint all laid out for the reforms that ought to take place in this neighborhood." Often you'll have to cover the same ground with a person or a group over and over again; often you'll have to take very small steps toward a far-off goal; often you'll have to work at getting a person or group to *see* and to *want* to do differently before they will even budge toward a new direction; sometimes your best-laid plans will flop like a house of cards. You must be willing to pace your steps to those of the people you work with; this is the necessity for any leader who is also a helper.

As for courage: mostly it is that the courage of your convictions must be firm and strong because they will often be challenged. They will be challenged not only by people "in power" who oppose what you propose to do but, often, even by the people with needs, whom you propose to help. You may find many kinds and sources of opposition to your plans or efforts. So you must be equipped both with such knowledge as underpins your convictions (and that is what professional education provides) and with the readiness to "stick your neck out" now and then and to take your chances.

Do you rate reasonably well? If so, come along further.

When a young social worker faces himself honestly on some morning when he is to meet his clients he sometimes

has qualms and says to himself: "Good heavens! What do I
know about what a marriage relationship should be like? Or
how a father should treat his delinquent son? Or what this
group of old people I am about to meet will think when they
see a callow youth like me?" Beginners in social work often
ask themselves these panicky questions: "How can I, barely
into my twenties, with a life experience that's been only
school, school, and more school—how can I know about and
help people with their problems? If I only had more experience . . ."

It is true that most beginning social workers are young and
have a rather limited range of life experience. But several
other things also are true. One is that you would have to live
a very long time to experience even a small part of the life
patterns and problems that are brought to social workers.
Another is that experiencing something does not necessarily
mean that one knows and understands it. (You know people
who have had many experiences but who see them simply as
"something that happened to me" and do not understand
them at all.) The reverse may also be true: that it is possible
to understand an experience deeply without having lived
through it. This is possible, however, only for those people
who have the ability we spoke of before—to give themselves
over to feeling into and with other people—and who, further,
always have their sensitive antennae out to get the meaning
and the sense of what is happening within their own small
life space.

What I am saying is that it is possible to have many real and
many vital vicarious experiences by the time you're twenty,
even if you're leading a so-called "sheltered life." It's possible if you've got your "feelers" out.

First of all, you have been part of a family. You have experienced the interactions between yourself and your parents and sisters and brothers and other relatives. You have been an observer of their actions and interactions. You have known sickness, maybe even death, and their effects on people. You have known happy moments and unhappy ones, and you can think back across your own life history enough to understand something of childhood and early adolescence and the kinds of things that affected you. You know something of the problems and pleasures of making friends and getting along with people, and something of the ways in which people can hurt and disappoint or help and support one another. You have had at least some small sample of almost all the human feelings there are to be felt. And while it is true that there is only one you and the people in your personal world are relatively few, human beings are enough alike so that you are already equipped to understand a good deal about them.

You have also had considerable experience with "social institutions" and the ways in which they affected you and others. Schools are social "institutions"; so are churches; so are hospitals and clinics; so are camps. You have experienced at least one of them. You have been aware—or a little thought can make you aware—of how their rules and policies, their atmospheres and programs have affected you and others like you in constructive or destructive ways. So you have a basic foundation for beginning to understand the impacts of social institutions as well as social conditions on the individual human being.

Thinking about and analyzing your own life experience and interactions with others is one way to begin to understand others. And there is a way to expand life experience itself. It is to read, read, read. Read novels, old ones, new ones, American, English, Russian—it doesn't matter. But they should be good ones, because a poor writer writes about paper dolls in contrived situations, but a good writer writes about three-dimensional beings caught up in conflicts within themselves or with others. If you can feel with the characters in novels and plays, if what they feel and think and do holds your interest, then you are having a kind of experience that widens and deepens your understanding of people and human dilemmas. Those who read a great deal and with depth have the good luck to experience many lives, not just one!

For a practical way to broaden your experience and to get some taste of what working with people is like look to summer jobs or once-or-twice-a-week volunteer jobs after school. In the summer, for college students, there are often these kinds of jobs available: camp counselors, playground or nursery school, or special education tutoring programs; some family and children's agencies, some mental hospitals, and many public assistance agencies will hire college students for the summer. After-school jobs or those for precollege students are most likely to be unpaid volunteer jobs, but they may offer interesting and valuable experience. They may be found in hospitals, reading to or playing with sick children and adults, in after-school tutoring or recreational programs with young people. Preference is usually given to college students, however.

For college sophomores and juniors who are seriously interested in exploring social work as a career, a number of welfare councils (by whatever name the organization of social welfare agencies in your community goes) have developed Careers in Social Work programs. They are summer programs of instruction and supervised work in selected social agencies and they pay a kind of scholarship, about $50–

$75 a week. Any one of your good local social agencies will be able to tell you whether or not a Careers in Social Work program exists in your community and, if it does, where to apply.

Now for the business of educational preparation and training to be a professional social worker. There are several choices you may make.

1. If you want to be a professional social worker, to make social work your career: You must have a master's degree from an accredited graduate school of social work in a university. The master's degree is awarded on your successful completion of two years (actually eighteen months) of classwork and supervised agency experience after your bachelor's degree.

COLLEGE COURSES   Most schools of social work will be more interested in the quality of your college undergraduate work and activities than in the exact roster of courses you took. Most schools would agree that a liberal education, a humanistic orientation, offers the best base for what the social worker must be and do.

Among the liberal arts and sciences are some subjects that bear closely on social work. They are required by many schools, valued by all, but under any circumstances they offer you a chance to see for yourself whether the subjects that are highly pertinent to social work have real interest for you.

Psychology, social psychology, biology, sociology, social anthropology—courses such as these provide explorations and explanations of man in interaction with his environment. You can see why they would be important.

Economics and political science courses offer the basic knowledge on which to build your understanding of government and its social welfare responsibilities; of the great public programs that are this country's major social services; of how an affluent society can have pockets of poverty; of what politics and taxes and government spending have to do with the man in the street who may be your client.

A course in statistics (don't groan!) offers you primarily tools for grasping what social work researchers and planners are talking about when they are trying to find out, for example, how widespread a problem is, what percentage of people are affected, etc. Social planning depends on such assessments.

Literature and philosophy courses deepen your understanding of human beings in conflict and dilemma. Literature opens ways of experiencing the lives of many other people; philosophy pushes you to think deeply about the human condition. Both exploration, in experiencing and in thinking, will broaden and deepen the reservoir of understanding you bring to social work education. Courses in writing and speaking are immediately useful. Social work is totally dependent upon communication, so its practitioners must know how to express themselves simply and plainly not only to their clients but to their colleagues, and especially to the community that supports their work.

It is not always possible to know in advance the language and its implied meanings of a particular client group. I say this because currently it is being suggested that the educated "middle-class social worker" cannot understand nor adequately communicate with a lower-class, ghetto-bound client. My response to this is *not* that we should provide lists of idiomatic words to social workers and have them memorized. It is rather that if a social worker is an attentive listener, if he asks people to tell him what they mean, if he shows them that he is interested in learning exactly what they are getting at, he will not only learn their special phrases and meanings but will earn their gratitude for his respectful attentiveness. The one foreign language that is useful in communities where there are numbers of Puerto Rican or Mexican clients is, of course, Spanish.

In the past ten years there has occurred in colleges throughout the country a virtual explosion of special courses and full sequences, or "majors," in social welfare. (The reasons for this are many but probably the main one is the almost sudden recognition by all Americans of the as yet unmet economic and social needs of large sectors of our population.) Thus there may be in the college of your choice (or your choice of a college may be affected by this) a liberal arts curriculum that is man-in-society oriented, that offers a number of courses toward understanding personal and social problems and the social provisions by which they can be met. These are discussed in some greater detail in the section that follows. Should you major in a social welfare sequence at college, your choice of a graduate school of social work should be carefully made so that you can be sure that your master's degree work will truly be at a higher level than what you've been exposed to in your college.

If you have gone through college with a major in some other sequence than the social or behavioral sciences, don't worry. Some chemistry and math and French majors have entered schools of social work and have done top-notch work. As yet no school will be closed to you because of your undergraduate course sequence. Most schools are chiefly interested in what you have done with the learning opportunities you have had.

GRADES   It is not possible to tell you what grade average you must have during your four years of college in order to enter a graduate school of social work. It varies. A few schools have all-university rulings about what grade average is the minimum for admission to any graduate school. Most schools are able to be flexible and will consider among other things the standing of the particular college that graded you (A's or C's from different schools are not always equal to one another, we know). They will also consider the grades in the subjects that relate most closely to social work and the circumstances in your student situation (such as working your way through school) that might have affected your scholarship.

But grades are not enough. Qualities of personality and your college interests and associations will be carefully considered for whatever light they may throw on your ability to invest your energies outside yourself and your freedom to work and play together with other people.

Schools of social work are not intent on getting only one kind of person. The fact is that many schools today are trying to study carefully who makes the best social worker, and what relation exists, for example, between academic success in college and success as a social worker, and between college activities and social work, and, beyond this, whether caseworkers, group workers, and community workers can be cut from the same cloth. Social work educators are sure they want a wide range of personalities, once the qualities mentioned at the beginning of this chapter are found to be present and once the undergraduate grades give evidence that the student can cope with what will lie ahead of him.

In the second half of your junior year at college you ought to begin thinking about where you'd like to go for your graduate work in social work. By the fall of your senior year you should have made the choice of the one or two schools to which you plan to apply. Your application should be in by January of your senior year (or of the year in which you hope to enter a school's fall program). Later applications are acceptable, of course, but early acceptance in the school of your first choice, scholarship grants, etc., go to the early bird. More on this later.

There are over seventy accredited graduate schools of social work today in the United States (including Puerto Rico and Hawaii) and Canada. (For their names and locations see Chapter Seven on where to find out more.) Some are relatively new schools, some old and long established; some are small, some quite large; some are in small college towns, some in big city university centers. Some have fairly high tuitions, and some (state university schools) have low tuitions for in-state students. Your choice will be affected by considerations of where you'd like to be geographically, school size and cost, and the descriptions of courses and aims you will find in their catalogues. You may also want to know about a school's reputation and standing (even though it is fully accredited). This information is a little harder to get, but your best bet is to discuss choices with any professional social workers you may know and with the sociology or other advisory faculty in your college. While it is true that graduation from certain schools has greater "prestige value" than from others, it is also true that an M.A. or an M.S. in social work from any accredited school opens the same doors—and many of them—to job opportunities.

When you have some idea of what school of social work you'd like to learn about, write to the dean or director for a catalogue. A careful reading of a school's catalogue gives you not only the facts noted in the paragraph above but other facts too, such as the particular advantages a school may have, the social agency connections it uses for student field-work, the scholarship of its faculty, and so on. Your choice may be affected by these factors.

APPLICATION   Wherever you apply, it is important that you apply early. This is because all schools of social work are now having an increase in applications, and even though each would like to take all qualified applicants, they must limit their enrollment. Enrollment is limited by the number of openings that social agencies are able to provide for the students' fieldwork, and when there are no more such field placements open, a school cannot take more students.

A second reason for being an early bird is that, while all schools have scholarship funds, no school has enough to meet all requests. (Scholarships will be discussed further on.)

Schools of social work are suffering from the same application problems that plague undergraduate colleges today: the multiple applications of one student to many schools. (Of course, that one student is only trying to leave no stone unturned in his motivated effort to achieve his goals!) But it becomes a costly process for a number of schools to go through the machinery that admission procedures involve so that one student can go to one school. Therefore, deans and directors of schools of social work would probably be in agreement that the prospective student should be asked to make as careful a preapplication choice as possible. Then apply to the two—at most three—schools that appeal to you for your own good reasons. If your applications go in sufficiently early, you will be notified soon enough of your rejection (should that happen) to be able to apply elsewhere.

When you get your application blanks you will find certain kinds of information asked of you. You will be asked for transcripts of your college record so that the courses you have taken and the grades given can be examined. You will be asked to give the names of people who would be willing to write reference letters about you. These should be people who have known you fairly well in their capacity as teacher or employer or professional acquaintance.

Many schools will ask you to write some account of how you happened to become interested in social work or what expectations you have of the field and of yourself in relation to it. Give this some careful thought. (One of the purposes of this book is to provide you with the food for such thought.) Try to write as honest and as open a statement as you can. Write a "this is what I, John Jones, am, want, feel, think" sort of answer rather than one of those "this is what I suppose you people want" letters. In the first sort of approach you come alive, you become a person for the people reading admission applications. In the latter approach you remain vague, dim, just another applicant. To show yourself as a person is important in a profession where so much hinges on interpersonal relationships.

Many schools like to have personal interviews with applicants. Of course, geographical distance often makes this impossible, and your inability to come for a personal interview will not stand in your way. To have your own questions answered, however, and to get some firsthand impressions of a school, you yourself might want to have a personal appointment with someone on the school's staff. Schools are glad to arrange for this.

SCHOLARSHIPS AND TUITION GRANTS All college and graduate work is expensive these days, and graduate work in a school of social work is no exception. Many parents today recognize that a bachelor's degree is no longer the entry to a vocation that it once was, and so they have planned and are ready to finance their young sons and daughters into graduate schools. If, however, financing is a problem for you, there are numerous possibilities for scholarship aids.

Most schools of social work give scholarship grants. Some cover full tuition plus expenses; some, tuition and partial expenses; and some, partial tuition only. The United States government, state governments, individual states, and individual agencies are willing to pour an astonishing amount of money into the education and preparation of good social workers. The need for social workers is great, and their usefulness is widely recognized. Many agencies give scholarships on condition that the recipient will pledge a year or two of work in those agencies following his graduation. Others give scholarship free of commitment in order to build up the manpower of professional social work.

The top priority for scholarships in most schools of social work today is for college graduates who are members of minority groups. Black students, Mexican-American, American Indian, Puerto Rican, students of Oriental origin—all these are being actively recruited and given first consideration by many schools of social work. You probably can readily see the reasons for this. You would expect schools of social work to be particularly sensitive to the need to provide opportunities to persons who have been socially disadvantaged. And you would also probably recognize that such persons, when well educated and skilled, might be able to be of particular help to those with whom their swift communication and basic identity occurs.

Every school's catalogue will tell you what particular scholarships and tuition aids it has to offer. Also, the Council on Social Work Education puts out a compilation of information about all social work education scholarships and money grants (see Chapter Seven).

Do not count on working while you are in a school of social work: it is possible but very difficult. A few students do manage it—if they have great energy and great self-discipline and are lucky enough to find a job that fits into a tight schedule. But you will find that going to a school of social work consumes more time and energy than you were accustomed to using in undergraduate work. This is partly because your practice "fieldwork" may take you far off campus, but it is mostly because fieldwork can take a lot of your physical and emotional energy. In a few instances fieldwork can be combined with earning money. (There will be many opportunities to get a summer job in social work between your first and second year of school.) But, by and large, schools encourage students to put themselves wholly and fully into the study of theory and practice that work in a professional school requires.

Now you have been accepted by a school of social work. Ahead of you lie two years of study and field practice. In prospect it seems a long time. You will find it will fly by breathlessly, so make the most of it right from the first!

The reason it takes two years for a master's degree in social work, while this degree may be won in many other fields in one year, is this: Classroom courses in social work are combined with actual practice in the field. All the kinds of agencies you read about in Chapter Four collaborate with schools of social work to provide placement for students. In these agencies social work students spend approximately half their time—about two and one half to three days a week—with the other half devoted to class courses.

The student caseworker (or group worker or community worker) carries cases (or groups or projects) with all the responsibilities of a staff social worker but on a more limited scale and with closer supervision. In your fieldwork you will try to apply and test all your class- and book-learned theories and principles. You will be finding that they "come true" with increasing frequency and deepened meaning for you. You will be putting your fast-growing knowledge to use in the service of people, learning to lend your eyes and ears and whole self to understanding, motivating, and assisting the people who are your clients. The constant safeguard that the school and the agency provide for you—and for your clients too—is the guidance, instruction, and constructive criticism of an experienced social worker who will be your fieldwork instructor.

It is not enough, as you can understand, for a student of social work to be academically competent. He must be this, but it is also necessary that what he is learning with his head be continuously transferred to his heart and his hand. He not only must know but must be able to do. So the student of social work is always being appraised by the quality of his classroom performance (which he is accustomed to) and also by his ability to put his knowledge to *use.*

Schools of social work that are in or near cities divide the week between in-school classes and off-campus fieldwork. Schools that are located in small communities with no range of social agencies use block placements. This means that they concentrate classwork on campus for several months at a time and then place students for months at a time in neighboring or far-off agencies. Each system has its advantages and disadvantages. Because it is not possible to say for a fact which is better, this consideration probably ought not to enter into your decision about what school to choose.

You will spend your first year's fieldwork in one agency. In your second year you will go to another type of agency, so that your experience of people and problems and social work places will be broadened. If you are a casework student, for example, you may spend your first year in a family welfare agency—public assistance or one of the voluntary family service agencies. In your second year you may choose your area of special interest—medical social work, advanced family casework, psychiatric social work, child welfare, and so on— and you will be placed in an agency in whose specialty you have particular interest. (A study of the catalogue of a particular school will tell you what kinds of agencies that school uses for its teaching centers.)

Your fieldwork days will give you an immediate experience of what it is like to be a social worker—you will not have to wait two years to find out. You will experience what it is like to carry the responsibilities of helping other people. (But give yourself time on this. You can't feel secure about it or do all the right things right from the start!) You will experience what a social agency is like as a place and as a purpose. You will have contact with many people besides your fellow students—other social workers, clerical people, psychiatric and medical consultants, administrators, as well as many people in the community outside. Your closest relationship will be with your field instructor (often called supervisor) who will be teaching and helping you and will always be in touch with the school about your progress.

On your "school days" you will be in the classroom, taking a sequence of courses designed to give you the foundation knowledge for social work. You may as well know now that there is not much free choice or many electives in a professional school's curriculum. Sometimes students who have enjoyed the freedom of range and choice in a liberal arts curriculum find themselves annoyed that in a school of social work they are required to take certain courses in a certain order, and that there is rarely time or space in their programs to sample attractive courses in other parts of the university. But this is a fact of life in any professional school: you are being prepared to be a member of a profession, and you are therefore required to take and to pass through its agreed-upon core of knowledge. A professional degree certifies that you have been taught, and have given evidence that you have incorporated, certain facts, theories, values, and skills. So with that firm (grim?) understanding, what will your course work consist of?

You will have a group of courses about human development from childhood through old age, about how the human being becomes "socialized" by the culture and conditions and institutions of his society, and about how social work (as one of those societal institutions) seeks to affect people's life circumstances so that they will be conducive to healthy growth rather than noxious. Along with these courses may be courses on the nature and dynamics of social groups and organizations (from the family up through governmental groups) with, again, emphasis upon how they are formed, operate, and their bearing on individual well-being.

A second major cluster of courses in all schools of social work has to do with the organization and nature of the social services. From these courses you will learn of the development of social work and social resources for the meeting of certain kinds of human need, the kind of provisions that have been developed to meet the economic, mental, and physical health, child welfare, and rehabilitation needs of people in our society.

You will study not simply what these are but how they

meet, or fail to meet, the social, physical, and psychological welfare of people; how politics and policies affect these services and what your state legislators and your congressman and your particular community have to do with them; what kinds of action are needed to make them better than they are; and what social workers have to do with making them more efficient and effective. You will find many questions of basic philosophy and social values involved, as well as many as yet unresolved issues; so here too, as in your methods courses, you will learn the facts by which to form your social opinions and will think about social action on the basis of these facts and opinions.

Another concentration of courses is in social research—courses that help you to learn and understand the basic conditions that must be met for valid fact finding and investigation of problems important to social work, and that give you some elementary practice in doing a piece of research. The intention is not to make a researcher of you; this would hardly be so easily achieved. The idea is rather to make it possible for you to spot and be able to formulate some of the problems in your profession that need to be studied, and to have some general idea as to what would be involved in making a study. Along with this, your courses in "social investigation" (or some equivalent title) aim to help you to become an intelligent "consumer" of research. Every day's newspaper reports on somebody's study that "proved" this or that, on some percentages or statistics that "show," for example, that employment is up or down, delinquency is more widespread in this group than in that, more fraud occurs in relief families than, etc., etc. The point is that public opinion is shaped and colored by these "facts" that are sometimes only half-facts and social programs are aided or hampered by them. The professional social worker ought to know how to read such "facts, figgers, and data," ought to be able to put a finger on where fallacies lie, if they are there, or to know what questions are yet to be answered. The social sciences, psychological and medical laboratories, and social work's own research centers are pouring out findings of all kinds that bear upon social work's programs and individual clients. How to appraise and use them is what your research sequence sets out to teach you.

Going along with these "knowledge and analysis" courses over the entire two years of your professional education will be the so-called "methods" courses—whether in casework, group work, community work, or combinations of them—are courses in which you study the theory and principles of "doing" as a professional social worker. They provide the whys and wherefores of what you do (or do not do) when and with whom. They show you the relationship between the skilled use of method and the underlying knowledge of the dynamics of human behavior as well as the dynamics of social systems. They show, too, the relationship between what a social worker does and his profession's commitments and values.

In the field—which is to say in your actual practice in some selected social agency—you will be having the direct experience of using yourself and your growing knowledge in the effort to help people deal with their problems or meet their felt needs. In fieldwork you try yourself out but also you try out your new-found learning in the "real life" situation. In this way fieldwork and classwork form a warp and woof of fabric of professional education, the weaving together of facts and theories and practice. Teaching you in the field, supporting you when you are unsure, helping you to connect social work's body of knowledge with the people and problems you are dealing with will be fieldwork teachers, working in collaboration with your classroom teachers.

Different schools at different times will have different single courses in their curriculums. Sometimes they are extra electives, sometimes required. But all schools of social work are agreed that their core courses are these that have been described and that give you knowledge on: man's makeup; his social interaction and functioning; the problems he creates or encounters; societal programs and provisions for man's needs; the processes social work has developed for solving the problems of man in society; the ways by which man's social welfare needs and the social services may be examined and appraised.

As I have presented these courses, it sounds as if they all come at once. They could not, of course. They extend over the two years' time, as you will see when you study school catalogues.

It is not all work and no play while you are attending a school of social work. At many schools, students form clubs that manage to provide both social work forums and social play. It is still possible to be involved in personal life and fun in campus activities and to take advantage of the rich and varied cultural opportunities that are to be found in many university communities.

Then one day you will be in that black gown with that awkward-fitting mortarboard balancing on your head again, being presented by your school for the university's M.A. or M.S. degree. The probability is that you will already have a job in your pocket. It is usual that in the last six weeks or so of your second year you will find out from your fieldwork agency and from your faculty advisor about job openings, or, as is often the case, you will have been found and interviewed by some agencies eager for trained and competent staff.

When you decide on "where," you'll find that there is a new beginning to make, new challenges, and that maybe you don't know as much as you wish you did. But you can surely know that at the very least you've got a firm base from which to learn and grow further.

2. If you want a social work job immediately on finishing college: To this point I've been talking about professional education for a career in social work that requires a master's degree. But it is possible that you are not sure you want to go on to graduate work. You may want to mature a bit first, or you may want to test yourself out in a real work situation, or you may not be able to afford more schooling until you work and save up some money. The fact is that there is an increasing number of jobs in social work and there is an unmistakable trend in the direction of welcoming into social work and making room for college graduates without full professional training.

In the past ten years there has been a considerable change in the thinking of social agencies and schools of social work about the potential man- and womanpower for social work that might be drawn directly from those whose education stops, whether finally or temporarily, with the B.A. degree. For a long time it had been thought that only professionally trained social workers held the knowledge and had the skills by which to attempt, responsibly, to influence other people. But two circumstances pushed their way into prominence, demanding some reconsideration of this earlier idea. One was the persistent manpower shortage in social work agencies, created chiefly by the tremendous expansion of social services that has occurred in these past few years when our society has become acutely aware of problems of poverty, of racial discrimination, of the paucity of opportunity in poor urban and poor rural areas. So various governmental and locally supported projects and agencies have sprung up all around, all aiming to ameliorate or modify or prevent the many problems of the poor and the near-poor, all needing, besides money and innovative ideas, the warm live bodies and minds to carry those ideas and programs into action. Professional schools of social work could not possibly provide the numbers of people necessary to man these projects and programs; at best they might provide some of the leaders and supervisors. The second realization came on the heels of observing how well "untrained" college graduates did with many of the people and programs with which they worked. Such programs as the Peace Corps and VISTA revealed their dedication, their interest, their imaginative and responsible coping with great varieties of personal and group and community problems.

Facing squarely up to these two realities the profession of social work has now placed before itself a major task: one, to try to identify what kinds of social services, what sorts of help can be properly and competently conveyed by young men and women with only a B.A. degree (and can be rewarding and gratifying to them too, enough so, perhaps, to motivate them to consider entering the professional social worker ranks at some later time). To these ends many agencies are today trying to plan and reorganize their programs to make fullest constructive use of social workers who come directly from college.

There has been strong political backing for the expansion of social work's manpower at the preprofessional level. In a

1967 amendment to the Social Security Act Congress authorized large sums of money for the development of training for social workers, at least half of which was to develop and expand programs in undergraduate colleges. With this impetus undergraduate curricula in social welfare and/or clusters of courses in this subject are literally snowballing. In 1965 there were 529 colleges giving such courses. When you read this there will possibly be double that number. (In the chapter "Where to Find Out More" you will find sources of exact information on the present-day situation.)

As of this writing there is a surge of sentiment in the National Association of Social Workers to admit into membership persons holding the baccalaureate degree in an accredited college if they have completed an undergraduate social welfare sequence. While the fate of this sentiment will be determined by a membership vote, it is significant that the all-professional organization has opened this possibility to consideration.

Meantime both the National Association of Social Workers and the Council on Social Work Education are bending their efforts to helping colleges design courses that will qualify students to carry certain social work tasks at the same time as they provide good liberal education. And meantime you may take such college courses in preparation for some work in the field of social welfare or simply in preparation for knowledgeable and responsible citizenship in the adult world.

The "good" undergraduate sequence, or "major," in social welfare is basically a good sequence of courses about man in his social environment. This is the essence of a "liberal education," actually: to understand man and society, to study what makes the human being develop in healthy constructive ways (or what thwarts that growth) and what forces and factors in society exists (or ought to exist) to offer the open opportunities to meet our human needs for security and self-realization. Good courses in literature bear on this; good courses in economics, sociology, political science, psychology—all show the connections between the individual human being and the other people and circumstances with which he is in transaction. Some social welfare majors in a number of colleges offer fieldwork observation and practice along with academic courses.

You should be aware, however, that there are some drawbacks, understandably, in entering the field of social service directly from college. These may be of a very temporary nature, but you may want to think them over. One is that the kinds of jobs you can get are not fully identified. This is because social agencies have not yet worked out what aspects of social service need the additional knowledge and skills that advanced education gives and what can be done with and for people "just as well" by the young college graduate. This is in work now. There are many tryouts in the use of "social work aides" or "paraprofessionals" or "social work technicians" who have only the B.A. degree, and out of such tryouts it is expected that full job identifications and specifications will emerge. Until that happens salary scales will probably not be formulated. Until that happens the "career ladder" remains rather ambiguous—that is, it is not clear whether it will be possible to work one's way up into more responsible and better paying jobs without graduate professional education. But one thing is certain: since a B.A. in an accredited college program in social welfare makes you admissible to a graduate program in social work (given an adequate record) and makes it possible for you to try yourself out in some part of social work's activities, you will have lost nothing and may have gained a good foothold toward a social work career.

3. If you plan only to finish junior college: Much of what has been said above holds for the student who thinks, right now, that he may not go much further than the end of junior college. (I say "right now" because your mind may change many times about future work or school plans, depending on grades and money and lots of other life circumstances.)

Not so long ago there would not have been any point in talking about going into social welfare work if you had only finished junior college. Today there is. Because of the recent great push in our country to offer welfare aids and social services to ghetto residents or other sectors of our disadvantaged populations, because of the development of neighborhood organization groups, community mental health, child education and care programs (such as Head Start), special helps to the aged, the retarded, the physically handicapped, there has been recognized the growing need for personnel to fill these present (or about to be instituted) jobs. The so-called "New Careers" movement is one in which the "community colleges" (that's the newer name for junior colleges) are investing considerable interest and planning in preparing young people or interested and capable adults to carry some parts of social welfare jobs. In a way this kind of preparation may be premature because *what* parts of *what* welfare jobs can be carried by people with only two years of college under their belts has not yet been settled or defined. On the other hand, it is argued, the best way of knowing how such people may best function is to try them out on the job. So community colleges are in the process of developing courses for "community service" aides.

It is estimated that there will shortly be several hundred community college programs (or two-year programs in four-year colleges) that will end in an "associate degree" in social welfare. The best of these programs will be those whose standards are high enough that they can lead to a four-year college degree and beyond should the student be able and wish to go forward with his education. There are many opportunities in these two-year programs to combine work and study; there are scholarships available for full-time study; and the expectation is that there will be additional governmental aids for tuition and living expenses.

There may be some real advantages to you in a job in social work if you cannot, or are not sure you want to, go directly on to graduate school. You will have the firsthand experience of all kinds of people in all kinds of trouble. You will be able to know and assess in yourself whether you are interested and willing to give yourself over to helping others in the best way you can. You will inevitably mature a bit in the process of working and of growing a year or two older. You may be able to save money for later schooling. You may be lucky enough to have a supervisor or administrator who is able to teach you and enhance your skills. You may be recommended for one of the agency scholarships to a school of social work in order to become a leadership person in the agency and the field. And if, as you work, you are doing everything you can to meet people's needs and lessen their hurts, then it will be an advantage to the people you serve that you are there.

But for them or their future counterparts, and for your own sense of identity and status and competence, hold before yourself the goal of full professional training.

When you are ready to come to some decisions—whether to try yourself out first in a community college social welfare program and get an "associate degree" or to enter a four-year college and take some social work-related courses or a major in social welfare towards your B.A. degree; whether on getting your B.A. degree you should go directly to graduate school for full professional training and status or work for a while first—talk these possibilities over carefully. Talk them over with your school's guidance counselor. If you know or can get in touch with a professional social worker, ask for his opinions and possible guidance. If you've gone as far as your junior year in college, talk or write to the admissions dean of a school of social work about your particular interests and assets. (And see Chapter Seven on how to find out more right now.)

Perhaps you have one more lingering but big question. It is the title of the next chapter.

six: **Why be**
a social worker?

Does it seem to you rather late in this book to be asking this question? I've held it until now on the notion that first you'd want to know the particulars of what you'd be involved in doing if you chose a social work career. Now that you have some idea—What's in it for you? What are the personal day-by-day satisfactions and the opportunities it will offer you?

First of all: Social work is where the action is. It is active engagement between you and other people. What you say and what you do will affect the lives of other people, either in your influence directly upon them or in your influence upon the social conditions that affect them.

Secondly: Social work is helping people. Again, as you've seen, it is helping them, one by one, to cope with their problems in social functioning, or it is helping them in or through group actions to deal with social conditions that create problems; and helping them, one by one, to achieve a more satisfying level of living or in and through groups to create more satisfying social conditions.

So, if being an active agent in helping people is your interest and motivation, that's the most important answer to "why."

Another thing: It is simply impossible for a social worker to be bored. The variety and interest and emotional impact of people of all ages, all backgrounds, involved in all the problems or the striving, all the hurts and the needs of human beings—this in itself keeps the social worker's daily job a lively, fascinating one. You are always with people, always related to life and living. Your work will bring you into contact and into working relationships with a number of other professional persons too—chiefly doctors, psychiatrists, teachers, often psychologists, lawyers, and various community leaders.

THE ADVANTAGES

As a social worker you are an instrument of potential help and change for the better in the lives of many people. They can and often do gain physical, mental, emotional, and sometimes even spiritual nourishment and strength from you and from the resources you can make available to them. There are many failures and disappointments in the outcome of a social worker's efforts, it is true, just as there are many sicknesses a doctor can do nothing about. But you will feel repaid, warmed in heart, when people respond to your help in ways that tell you they feel better, as a result of your help, or more capable of shouldering their own load. A smile that breaks across the face of a child whose inner tensions had once frozen him, a grudging but sincere "thanks a lot" from a troubled adolescent, a former psychotic patient who says, "I'm not afraid to go home to my family now," a group that has learned to govern itself and put its combined energies into constructive action—any and all of these are rich rewards to the social worker. They say that you, in some small way, have helped someone to be and to do better.

You will know firsthand, will be able vicariously to experience many lives beyond your own. Not only will your world become peopled with a great variety of human beings, good and bad, with problems that are distressing, with courage that is heart-lifting, but because of your front-line knowledge of community conditions your daily newspaper will come alive for you. You will suddenly have an investment in whether the School Board votes yea or nay on some issue, in what the mayor or the City Council decides to do about urban renewal, in whether taxes should be used for this or that project. You will, in short, become an involved, interested, and therefore an *interesting* person. (And on some days you may even sigh and wish to heaven you had a more monotonous job!)

"To serve" is probably the most important motive in social work—to reach out a hand to a fellow man—whether in one's own country or in a foreign land, whether on a person-by-person basis or through planning and execution of community reforms. When that service or help yields some fruitful results, even modest ones, the feeling of being lined up on the side of humanness and of man's welfare is a deeply satisfying one.

THE NEED

Probably never before in the history of the world have so many people been so sincerely concerned about the well-being and the right to self-realization of every man. Never before have the poor been so "visible," have concerns about the pockets of hunger and deprivation in this country been so widely known and discussed, have feelings about the rights of the dispossessed been so high. Never before have young people in high schools and colleges involved themselves so deeply in feeling and understanding the unmet needs of people in the crowded ghettos or in the hollows of the Appalachian Mountains or the worn-out plantations and small farms of the South. There are many reasons for our general and acute awareness of human needs that cannot be dealt with here. The result, however, is that there has been a great burgeoning of social welfare programs in the effort to meet these varied needs and, of course then, a greatly increased demand for social workers. (In a report issued by the U.S. Department of Health, Education, and Welfare in 1965 it was anticipated that by 1970 their programs alone would need 100,000 professionally prepared social workers plus a vast number of social workers whose college or junior college work would prepare them as "aides" and "technicians.")

It is an interesting phenomenon that the more affluent a society the greater the recognition of and need for social workers seems to become. This is because as a society raises its standards of living peoples' standards of expectations rise accordingly. The "poverty" in the United States would be considered "riches" by populations in parts of India or Africa, for instance. The more a society meets the basic bread and shelter needs of its citizens the more people become aware of their rights to "life, liberty, and the pursuit of happiness." They begin to be able to look up from their mere survival needs to say, "There are other rights I have too"— such as the right to expect happiness in marriage or the right to expect recreational and educational opportunities for oneself and one's children to expand the horizons of life satisfactions. Therefore, social workers are needed and sought to provide services beyond those required to keep body and soul together: to give counseling on problems in marriage on parent-child difficulties; to help children do better in school and to work with teachers to make the schools themselves better for children; to offer leisure-time activities that occupy people with others and bring out their latent talents; and so on. In short, as long as we live in a society that values the individual human being and believes in his capacity to become more than he is now, both as a private person and as a citizen of the community, so long will that society want social workers, among its other professions, to make that goal possible.

Thus when you enter social work you enter an expanding field of service. (Incidentally, human services to human beings cannot be automated, so there is little danger that the knowledge and skills you develop will become obsolete or be taken over by a new machine!)

JOB OPPORTUNITIES AND BENEFITS

If you graduate from a school of social work with a master's degree, there are usually about eight to ten openings you will be able to choose from. (Of course, how many agencies want you and how much they want you depends in part on your references and recommendations as a student.) They are in family and child welfare agencies, in psychiatric and medical clinics and hospitals, in school systems, juvenile courts, children's institutions, settlement houses, community mental health clinics, councils of community agencies, and some (as yet hard to classify) emerging organizations for grass-roots community development.

These opportunities occur from Maine to California and in far-off places (Alaska, Hawaii, Puerto Rico) and in Canada, and sometimes in foreign countries (though these latter are usually for social workers with some experience).

Most openings are still for social caseworkers, that is, for those who are trained to help individuals and/or their families with some problems in their daily functioning. (The fact seems to be that even those social workers who set out to be community group organizers or to work with groups for specific social action reforms find that many of the people they've gathered together have personal problems that need immediate attention before the social problem in the large can be dealt with—so even community workers often find themselves involved, willy-nilly, in casework.) But there is a growing demand for social workers who have skill in both work with individuals (casework) and work with small groups, families or problem-centered groups (group work), and increasingly schools of social work are offering some theory and experience in both methods. A parallel situation is that of the seeming need to combine the social action-decision making operations of community work and group work. Several schools are experimenting with this combined specialty in the anticipation that job specifications in community centers and social action organizations will be calling for these fused skills.

Salaries for the professionally educated social worker have risen remarkably over the past ten years. In 1959 the National Association of Social Workers recommended to the employing agencies that the beginning salary for an inexperienced graduate from a school of social work should be $5,400 per year. Today's recommendation (not yet fully achieved, but almost, as the job advertisements later will show you) is $10,-500. A National Association of Social Workers' survey reported on in May, 1969, reveals that the median salary of professional social workers as of 1968 was $11,184. ("Median," you will remember, means the middle point in a range and that there are as many salaries *above* as *below* it.) This figure includes all employed social workers, of course, not just beginners. The median reported in 1960 was $7,000, so that means that in eight years it has risen by over $4,000.

Salaries not only vary by the type of employing agency but are higher or lower in different parts of the country. Sometimes they are lower where actual costs of living are lower. Sometimes they are lower where living costs are high, but where climate and scenic beauties or cultural advantages make up for less money. The struggle to get agency boards and Community Chests and legislative bodies to pay adequately for the social workers they want will be a continuing one, but there have been remarkable results in the past few years. The steady rise of social work salaries reflects the recognition by communities not only of the need for social work but of its value.

The "fringe benefits" in social agencies are, as you might expect, socially responsible and generous. Paid vacations are usually four weeks a year. Sick leave and pregnancy allowances, insurance and pension plans are usually sound and good. Social workers are encouraged to take time out for ongoing study, to take special courses for the advancement of their professional skills (often with fees paid by their agencies), and to attend national conferences on social welfare matters (again with travel expenses often provided by the agency).

In the several pages that follow you will find some actual advertisements for job openings for caseworkers, group workers, community workers, and some for just "social workers" who are asked to be able to operate by more than one process—to be caseworkers able to do group work, or group workers able also to do some casework, or community workers able to do (one wonders who can qualify!) whatever needs doing. You will notice that these openings all ask for (or imply the necessity for) a master's degree. I have omitted the exact locations and agencies and some irrelevant (to you) details but otherwise the ads are as they appeared these past few months in the National Association of Social Workers' bulletin, *Personnel Information.*

CASEWORK

By far the greatest numbers of openings and employment opportunities are in this category.

CASEWORK THERAPIST. For established metropolitan community treatment facility with stable staff. Therapy primarily with adults experiencing marital, personal, and parent-child problems and with adolescents. Psychoanalytically oriented consultation and ongoing staff development program includes psychiatric and casework seminars. The usual treatment modalities are available including family therapy, group therapy, and community consultation. Applicant must have MSW (or comparable preparation) with strong desire for clinical practice and training. Will consider person with little or no experience who has potential. Excellent personnel practices. Salary range up to $15,000.

CASEWORKERS. Immediate openings in well-established and expanding agency for casework therapy with families of retarded children. Interdisciplinary approach. Provides psychiatric clinic, special training programs for retarded children from infancy through school age, individual and group counseling for parents, research program, and comprehensive staff development program. Psychiatric and psychological consultation. MSW required. Salary $8,500–$11,000, depending on qualifications and experience.

FAMILY THERAPIST. Casework focused on crisis intervention, marital, parent-child, and social adjustment problems. Staff seminars, psychiatric consultation, and progressive supervision plan. Opportunity to develop skill in direct casework treatment of children and to participate in family life education program. Master's degree required. Liberal personal practices, social security. Salary range $7,775–$10,940.

PSYCHIATRIC SOCIAL WORKERS (2). To function in a developing and expanding comprehensive community mental health clinic. Current staff consists of 3 psychiatrists, 3 psychologists, 3 social workers. Current emphasis on working with schools and other agencies in program development. A dynamic program. Required: MSW; beginning worker with limited experience. Salary range $8,900–$10,400.

CASEWORKER. Service to Unmarried Parents Department in multifunction agency serving all races in a total program including own maternity homes. Unmarried mother work is family oriented, includes many adolescents, and provides pre-and postnatal counseling. Psychiatric and psychological consultation, seminar program, group counseling. Opportunity to practice at highest creative level. MSW required. Salary scale $8,400–$12,500.

GROUP WORK

GROUP WORKER. For residential program in multifunction children's agency. Responsibilities include organizing and supervising activities program and working with volunteers. Trained professional staff and psychiatric consultation. MSW required. Good fringe benefits. Salary commensurate with experience. Starting rate $7,800.

SOCIAL GROUP WORKER. Work hard, think hard, make an impact. Join 7 excited, innovating MSW group workers seeking new appropriateness in their services to children. Treatment-oriented groups based in the community have been used for over 10 years. A pace-setting private agency whose contributions to the child welfare field have been creative and substantial in re-evaluating its service patterns. Unwed mothers, juvenile delinquents, foster care, adoption, children who are emotionally conflicted are the reasons for the search for new answers. Excellent personnel policies and fringe benefits (e.g., 5 weeks' annual vacation). Salary $8,000–$12,500.

GROUP WORK EXTENSION SUPERVISOR. In a neighborhood center serving a community of 50,000 with emerging problems. Challenging opportunity to work with middle and lower middle-income families. Diversified agency with intensive group work program. Dynamic professional staff supported by informed board of directors and wide variety of community resources. Extension worker supervises extension program in 5 neighborhoods throughout the city, 2 of them interracial. MSW desired, but will consider other degree with some previous experience. Major medical, Blue Cross, and the like paid by agency. Liberal personnel practices. Many cultural advantages in metropolitan area. Salary range $7,000–$8,500.

GROUP WORK SUPERVISOR. Group work supervisor will have responsibility for theoretical and practical leadership in the area of planning and programing for preadolescents and adolescents afflicted with rheumatic fever and juvenile rheumatoid arthritis who are being treated in a day hospital service. Position calls for creative thinking and flexibility in the early stages of developing group process. Salary range $8,500–$11,500.

GROUP WORKER. You always say that community centers and straight recreation work do not fully utilize your treatment skills. Well, we would like you to use what you have been trained to do. We are looking for someone who can come in and lead 4 cottage groups of 12 children each, be in the cottages, and use himself to stimulate positive human relationships. We have a psychiatrist, psychologist, group workers, and caseworkers. If you like, come and look us over.

COMMUNITY WORK

COMMUNITY ORGANIZER. To coordinate activities of strong neighborhood group of Willow's Model Cities program. Ability to supervise staff and assist with planning and implementing needed programs. Minimum requirements are a degree in social sciences or community organization and related experience.

MODEL CITIES SOCIAL PLANNER. In a medium-sized urban community. We are presently entering the second year of Model City planning. United Community Services is helping in the planning and development of a social service system related to the total plan for model neighborhood. Funds for this position are provided jointly by United Community Services and the Model Cities agency.

COMMUNITY ORGANIZERS. To assist communities in prevention and control of juvenile delinquency with special emphasis on community involvement of youths in problems of youth. MSW required. Salary $8,550–$10,000.

COMMUNITY ORGANIZER. For three year demonstration program. Block organization, self-help project for housing, welfare, education, employment. MSW required. Liberal fringe benefits. Salary $8,000–$11,000.

"GENERALIST" SOCIAL WORKER

Here you will see some of the "crosscuts" of practice occurring in agencies that are seeking to offer help to help needers by whichever of social work's present-day processes (casework, group work, community work) seem most called for.

GENERIC SOCIAL WORKER (MSW). We are expanding our health care program for low-income families and are searching for qualified personnel. This new program is sponsored by a well-established, progressive 165-year-old group practice medical care program with 15 physicians including those in the major medical specialties. It is funded mainly by the OEO neighborhood health centers program. Our outreach staff includes a cadre of indigenous visiting health aides, public health nurses, community organizer-health educator, and social worker. We are currently expanding our staff significantly to handle increased enrollment of families in the program. A social worker is needed to help develop new ways of delivery of service to low-income families. Opportunity to use casework, group work, and community organization skills with a congenial and flexible staff. Some direct work with families as well as consultation with visiting aides and nursing supervisors and participation in program planning and administration. Psychiatric consultation readily available. A mental health program is being planned as part of the expansion of our program. Beginning salary up to $12,-000, depending on experience, with $500 annual increments to $14,000.

PROGRAM DIRECTOR. Needed for challenging job in a predominantly black community. Position requires supervision of staff, involvement of neighborhood volunteers, and contact with a variety of community action groups. MSW preferred. Excellent personnel practices.

SCHOOL SOCIAL WORKER. For surburban school system 40 minutes from Chicago Loop. ACSW supervision, psychological evaluation, psychiatric consultation; excellent special education program. MSW required. No teaching experience or training required. Travel allowance, teacher tenure, and retirement. Salary $7,700–$12,000 for 9½-month school year.

SCHOOL SOCIAL WORKERS. Planned program expansion to meet the needs of an increasing school population allows us to add 2 MSW's in either casework or group work to our existing staff of 7. The agency serves children in both regular and special education programs. Individual and group treatment. New and recent MSW graduates. Ten-month work-year. Salary begins at $9,000 for new graduates in a range to $14,000. Annual increments up to $500.

IMMEDIATE opening in community psychiatric clinic for psychiatric social worker (salaries dependent on experience, up to $11,172). MSW required. Clinic has long-established program of outpatient service to metropolitan area. Beautiful, contemporary facilities. Affiliation with university in training of social workers, psychologists, psychiatrists, psychiatric consultation, or other specialists as needed. Development of individual style in work valued highly. Comprehensive community mental health concept is basic and soon to be augmented with inpatient and 24-hour emergency service. Wide scope of function with variation in assignment based on individual interest and program necessity. Excellent personnel practices: 4 weeks' vacation, private practice privilege, health insurance, other favorable benefits.
Adult Division: Psychotherapy with adults, group treatment, brief treatment, crisis-oriented intervention.
Children's Division: Intensive individual and group psychotherapy, work with families. Case load of adolescent and younger boys.

After about three years of experience (and depending, of course, on your agency's needs and your competence) many other aspects of social work employment will be open to you. Supervisory positions where you teach younger workers or students, executive or administrative jobs as director of small agencies or of large agency departments, special demonstrations and experiments in practice—all of these wait to be filled by social workers who have proved their competence in practice.

Many social workers prefer not to supervise or "administer" because they most enjoy the direct work with their clients, individuals or groups. Direct practice is, indeed, the lifeblood of any profession. As agency boards have grown to recognize this, salary adjustments have been made so that today many agencies have no difference between their top practitioners' salaries and those of their supervisory or administrative staff, and the social worker who wants to continue as a caseworker or a group worker may do so without loss of money or prestige.

Increasingly, though still in small numbers, professional social workers are returning to those schools of social work which give advanced study to work for their Ph.D. or D.S.W. (the former is an "academic degree," held equivalent to all other Ph.D.'s within the university; the latter, a doctor of social work, is a "professional degree"). Study for either one is for those professionally competent social workers who wish to turn to teaching and research in university schools of social work or who wish to qualify for research leadership in social work. With occasional exceptions the candidate for a Ph.D. or D.S.W. is expected to have had several years of post-master's degree direct practice (in which he showed himself competent). This is in the belief that he who teaches or studies should *also* be able to *do* and should know his subject matter not just "in the head" but experientially too. But this is still a long way off for you.

In the meantime, "to serve," "to help" is probably the most

important motive in becoming a social worker, the basic answer to the question "why?" To reach out to a fellow human being or to a group of persons who need help, to be an active agent in making something happen that is better for human life rather than worse is to give one a feeling of being lined up on the side of humanness and human welfare. Even when you cannot always achieve your utopia or your dream for one individual person there is great gratification in stretching toward it.

Suppose you cannot yet decide whether or not to go on to a graduate school because you are uncertain about whether you want to make a career of social work or for other reasons. There is a growing number of job opportunities in social work for people with only a bachelor's degree and even for people who are (decisively or temporarily) ending their formal education at the end of junior college. These openings and the preparation required for them are discussed in the chapter on how you get to be a social worker. Here it can be said, however, that if the human relationship satisfactions mentioned above appeal to you, then you should consider them as an important reason for entering some form of social service.

FOR MEN ONLY

Social work in all its forms needs men. It needs men for a lot of reasons. Many of the toughest social problems are those that call for a man-to-man approach. Growing boys who have never known a father, boys who have known only harsh, punishing, or irresponsible men as fathers, delinquent youths and street gangs, male alcoholics and drug addicts, men who have had their hope and aspirations drubbed out of them by chronic underemployment or "bad luck"—all these need a man, as their caseworker or group worker, to identify with, to feel at one with, and take on as a kind of "model." Women social workers do work with all such men and boys, to be sure, and often with good results, but the psychological fact is that there are certain qualities of "manliness" or "manhood" (just as there are of womanliness and womanhood) that make contact and relationship easier and often more potent particularly with a troubled member of the same sex. So for all kinds of casework and group work services, steady, stable, warmly relating men are in great demand.

Let's face it—it's a man's world even in social work. Given equal competence a man is more likely to be promoted or chosen for executive, administrative, and public relations jobs than his female counterpart. (Mostly, however, the women seem to want it that way!) It is a fact that advancement for competent young men in social work is very rapid, and that men's salaries usually top those of women in equal positions. Partly this is because men are assumed to be responsible for providing for a family—or to be preparing for such responsibility. Partly it's because men have been in great demand and in scarcer supply.

Men are especially valued, too, for administrative and executive jobs that involve working with groups of men in other professions or in business. The major community organization jobs are carried by men, and increasingly men are being sought to head social agencies and special social work projects.

In brief, the whole field of social work is cordial and open and eager to use and reward the talents of capable young men and to offer them many opportunities. About one third of the membership of the National Association of Social Workers is male.

FOR WOMEN ONLY

If you've read the preceding section you may be feeling wounded that again men and boys seem to have the edge on women in our society. But cheer up, there's still lots of room at the top in social work for the woman who chooses it as her career. Moreover, it offers some very special benefits to women.

We assume in social work that a young woman looks forward to marriage and motherhood as part of her natural development as a woman. Not everyone achieves these roles, for lots of reasons, and if one remains unmarried, or is divorced or widowed, or is married and childless, the advantages of having a profession to pursue are clear to be seen. But what if you do get married and have a family—is there any point in going through the rigors and expense of professional preparation for social work? The answer seems to be an enthusiastic "Yes!" to judge by the reactions of many young and middle-aged married women in social work today.

First of all, education for social work is by its nature education for living in good relationships with other people. What you learn in social work courses and field experience about the dynamics of the human personality and behavior, about the ways people create and can be helped to solve their problems—these will cast many new lights on your own behavior and on the ways in which wifehood and motherhood can be sustained and developed as happy and healthy experiences. Many of the young women who marry right after college and who, as they say, plan to "work my husband's way" through his prolonged schooling or until his job yields better salary attest to the personal values schooling in social work has had for them. But this is only "by the way."

Many young women today, though married, continue to work. Sometimes it is for financial reasons. In social work it is often for reasons of the "pull" in the work: it is vital, important, interesting. (Secret: It makes even more interesting conversation with your husband than what you said to the butcher when he tried to overcharge you!)

When babies come you may want to leave work and give yourself over fully to being a mother. This is good. But the day may come—after your children go off to school, perhaps—when you want to reach out for refreshment and intellectual stimulation. If so, you may be able to find part-time work in a social agency. Increasingly social agencies are hiring professionally trained and experienced married women for limited hours or days per week.

When you reach middle age (if you can think that far ahead) and your children go away to school or to live elsewhere, you can, with a refresher course or two, return to your career. The common plaint of the middle-aged mother today is that she has nothing to do with herself, "now that the children no longer need me." Often she casts about frantically and futilely to find some interest or function for herself. The woman who has a profession, even though she may have retired from it temporarily, has something to go back to—she has a future.

There are many jobs in social work where women are especially valued: work with adolescent girls, unhappy or delinquent; with little children who need "mothering persons"; with unmarried mothers and with adoptive parents; with groups of girls trying to develop social and occupational competences; with mothers of problem children and wives in unhappy marriages. Again, this is not to say that a woman social worker deals only with children and female clients. She has many men clients too. And she often works in collaboration with men colleagues of her own or other professions (doctors and psychiatrists, for example). But there are some special kinds of human wants where the mothering capacities of a woman are most useful and much valued.

For women social work offers a career that can, with some managing, be combined with careers as wife and mother; offers work that is useful, alive, challenging, and that enriches your personal life.

Now, in full honesty, I must tell you about some of social work's disadvantages.

You will never get rich in social work. The greatest majority of social workers are and always will be salaried employees of either governmental or voluntarily supported agencies. Since those salaries come from taxes or community contributions and since, like education, social work is "nonprofit" making, you can see why salaries are likely to be modest to adequate. Another reason for its middling salary range is that the profession of social work does not yet have the prestige and status of some other professions, particularly law and medicine. There are a number of reasons for this. One is, as I have said before, that social work in its professional form is young, and while it is wanted it does not have the "market value" of some older professions.

Moreover, social work has had to live down its reputation as an occupation of volunteer "do-gooders." Because social workers have been the champions of the poor and the hurt and the "losers" in our society they are a kind of social conscience. Nobody really loves his conscience (though he may *respect* it) and so there is some reluctance to pay it well, in either money or status. But perhaps most important in the holding back of prestige and monetary rewards in social work has been that so many people who "do social work" and are called "social workers" have not had professional education and do not hold the graduate degree that designates "professional." There remains some confusion in the public mind about what expertise it should be paying for.

Yet, with all of this, there is more recognized need and clamor for social workers than ever before in our history. And along with this has come increasing respect, especially for the professionally prepared social worker, and, in the past five years, a steadily rising salary scale.

Still on the subject of social work's disadvantages, so that you may enter it with both eyes wide open: should you become a social worker you will find that you are often having to explain yourself and your profession to other people— sometimes to hostile ones, sometimes to friendly ones. You will have to explain "just exactly what it is you do" time and again. You will interpret over and over that all people who are poor are not, a priori, cheats and chiselers. You will find yourself at a dinner party explaining to the person on your right why social workers deal with the social problems of middle-class people as well as of the poor and to the person on your left why social workers must champion the rights of the underdog. In short, social work is frequently under fire and challenge, and it calls for conviction and clarity in its practitioners to win its prestige.

Finally, among social work's disadvantages is the fact that social work is not an easy job: it is not a nine-to-five proposition, though these may be your actual working hours. A social work job takes a lot of energy, physical and psychological, if only because of the self-discipline that is involved in dealing with a great variety of people who are so often under stress or in crisis. Its problems may wake you in the middle of the night, when you may start up thinking: Heavens- I should have done this—or that- Or: I wonder if Sally really did go home instead of to her boy friend's. Or your involvement in some social-political issue or some agency problems may keep you at a committee meeting far into the night. Many times social work requires that you be able and willing to extend yourself beyond yourself.

Why be a social worker? Chiefly because social work is more than a job. Its material rewards are modest, to be sure, and its frustrations are many. But its personal, intellectual, "inner-growth" rewards are rich. You will be in the mainstream of the life of man, in the hurly-burly of everyday living and its problems. You will be using yourself—your knowledge and your personality—as an instrument of help to people with needs and often with hurts. You will be challenged to lift your eyes from what you do every day to envision and plan what might be done to bring about a better society.

That deeply human scientist, Albert Einstein, once wrote:

Strange is our situation here upon earth. Each of us comes for a short visit, not knowing why, yet sometimes seeming to divine a purpose. From the standpoint of daily life, however, there is one thing we know: That Man is here for the sake of other Men. ... Above all, for those upon whose smile and well-being our own happiness depends, and also for the countless unknown souls with whose fate we are connected by a bond of sympathy. Many times a day I realize how much my own outer and inner life is built upon the labors of my fellow men, both living and dead, and how earnestly I must exert myself in order to give in return as much as I have received.

If you respond to this, if wholeheartedly you feel like saying, "Yes! I believe that too!"—then the profession of social work is for you.

As I write these lines there are to be heard all about us the ominous rumblings of missiles and rockets and exploits into outer space. It occurs to me that social workers are among the few groups left who stubbornly affirm the importance of *inner* space. They are intent upon the inner well-being of man so that he can carry his daily life roles as a student or worker or spouse or parent with a modicum of personal pleasure and social adequacy. They are intent upon the inner space of family life so that it can be made the soil for the growth and development of reasonably happy persons who are also reasonably responsible citizens. They are concerned with the inner space of the inner city—to wipe out the conditions that corrode the lives of its people and supplant them by conditions that sustain and enrich good human development. In the final analysis these various levels of the inner space of human life must be your major interest if you think of being a social worker. You will surely not be able to solve all the problems; but just as surely you will be part of a goodly company, past and present, of those who affirm the worth of man here on earth. This is the basic "why" of social work.

seven: **Where to
find out more**

In this chapter you will find specific leads and information about where you can find out more, whether about schools of social work or social work jobs or any other particular questions you may want answered about social work in general.

Your first and best over-all source of information, the National Commission for Social Work Careers, is set up especially to interest young men and women in social work, to recruit them into the field, and toward that end to inform them of both the requirements and the opportunities in a social work career. It is located at 2 Park Avenue, New York, New York 10016.

A letter to them will bring you information such as the following:

1. On schools of social work: the names and addresses of the seventy-plus accredited schools in the United States and Canada.
2. On career opportunities: the Commission has kits of infor-

mation set up especially for high school students, for college students, for college graduates, and (you may want to pass this information along) for school counselors. Tell the Commission which one you are interested in. (And ask about the price. Costs and prices change, so I am not quoting them here. Most *single* copies of material will be sent to you free by the Commission but kits and packets must be charged for to cover costs.)

3. A list of places around the country that have special programs to interpret social work to interested students and/or to give them some tryout experience in it. "Careers in Social Work," for instance, is a program carried in a number of cities where during the summer qualified college students are given paid placements in social agencies along with training in order to get a taste of the field and to test their interest and aptitudes.

First step is to write to the National Commission asking for their free order form and publication list.

About Schools and Scholarships

The Council on Social Work Education, 345 East 46th Street, New York, New York 10017, will send you the following information:

1. A list of names and addresses of the colleges and universities in the United States that give *undergraduate* courses and sequences in social welfare *and* are members of the Council. (Cost: about 10 cents. Check with the Council.)

2. A list of accredited graduate schools of social work. (This is the same as the one the Commission will send you. Cost as above.)

3. A booklet: *Student Financial Aid for Master's Programs in*

Graduate Schools of Social Work in the U.S.A. and Canada.
(Ask, when you write, what the price of this is. It is probably
close to $2. Your college job counselor's office may—or should
—have it.) Actually, any school of social work to which you
may apply will inform you of its special free scholarship and
loan funds.

About 85 percent of all students in graduate schools of
social work are getting some part or whole financial aid for
tuition and expenses today.

The community's need and wish for fully or partly trained
manpower for social work is nowhere better shown than in
the large amounts of money being poured in to meet the
tuition payments and going-to-school costs of students. Scholarships are being provided by the United States government,
by various social agencies themselves, and by foundations
and interested individuals.

Scholarships are particularly available to qualified students
of minority groups—for students of Latin or Mexican background, for Black students, American Indians, those of Oriental origin—so that they may meet the great and special needs
of their ethnic groups.

As has been said, there is widespread heightened and has-
tened interest in the preparation of people for paraprofessional and social work aide jobs by community colleges and
undergraduate social welfare programs. The best sources of
information about what scholarship aid is available is your
school's career or guidance counselor. If you are in a four-
year college, talk to one of the faculty teaching in the social
welfare sequence about possible scholarship aid if you need
it to carry you through the program.

About Social Work in General

The *Encyclopedia of Social Work* is the best one-volume source book for "all about social work." In it you will find articles about all the kinds of social agencies there are, the special fields of social work practice, the history of social work, the names and addresses of national organizations that can give you detailed and current information about their programs, and so on. The present encyclopedia was published by the National Association of Social Workers in 1965; a new edition is due in 1971. Your school library or public library ought to have it, because it is a small gold mine of information and guidance on almost every question you may have about social welfare and social work.

About Social Work Practice

If you'd like to read more about casework or group work or community work, perhaps to help you make a choice of which method you would like to specialize in if you go on to graduate school, the following books (which should be in your college or public library) will give you a deeper understanding of each.

CASEWORK

1. *Helping: Charlotte Towle on Social Work and Social Casework*, ed. Helen Harris Perlman. Chicago: University of Chicago Press, 1969.

2. *Social Casework: A Problem-Solving Process*, Helen Harris Perlman. Chicago: University of Chicago Press, 1957.

3. *Theory and Practice of Social Casework*, Gordon Hamilton. New York: Columbia University Press, 2nd ed., 1951.

GROUP WORK

1. *Social Work with Groups,* Helen Northen. New York: Columbia University Press, 1969.

2. *Social Group Work: A HLPING Process,* Gisele Konopka. Englewood Cliffs, N.J.: Prentice-Hall, 1963.

3. *Essentials of Social Group Work Skills,* Helen A. Phillips. New York: Association Press, 1957.

COMMUNITY WORK

1. *Community Problem-solving: The Delinquency Example,* Irving A. Spergel. Chicago: University of Chicago Press, 1969.

2. *Community Organization: Theory and Principles,* Murray G. Ross. New York: Harper & Row, 2nd ed., 1967.

3. *Slums and Community Development,* Marshall B. Clinard. Glencoe, N.Y.: Free Press, 1966.

About Jobs

Of course job opportunities—summer part-time and volunteer—will vary from one community to another. And, of course, college upperclassmen and college graduates will have more chances than younger or less well-prepared people.

If you live in a city that has a coordinated careers or manpower program or some kind of welfare council or United Fund or Community Chest organization (these are usually not only fund-raising but also over-all social planning organizations), an inquiry directly to them will give you leads to possible openings in the local agencies that affiliate with them. Such agencies (called "voluntary" because they are supported by people's voluntary contributions) consist of far and child care agencies, youth-serving agencies, programs for the aged, and so on. Many of these agencies are organized on a national basis but only their local offices in the geographical area in which you want to work can tell you whether they have job openings. So you'll have to do a patient, dogged job of getting in touch with the agencies in your community and telling them of your interest and qualifications or making your inquiries.

For work in public (which is to say, tax supported) agencies you may take several paths: Ask for an appointment with a counselor in the local office of your State Employment Services; a number of employers are registering their social welfare jobs there. In your public library you will find a copy of the Directory of State Merit Systems which lists location and addresses of places where civil service examinations may be given for various jobs. Such jobs may be in the public assistance agencies, in public child welfare programs, hospitals for the retarded and the mentally ill, correctional schools for young offenders—agencies and services of many kinds. There are also many recently organized programs under the war on poverty auspices—programs of tutoring, child care, job training, various sorts of rehabilitation. (Because these are so frequently subject to change, depending on federal and local fund appropriations and a community's satisfaction or discontent with the program, their existence and their job openings must be checked at the time of your interest.)

If you would prefer to get a job outside the area in which you live, in some other part of the country, your best bet, probably, is to find out from one or more national organizations what *local* agencies they have in the area you want to work in. Be clear: the national organization will not be able to tell you where and whether there are employment opportunities in local agencies. It can only tell you where to apply to find out.

The best place to get the names of national agencies (such as Boys' Clubs of America, the National Federation of Settlements and Neighborhood Centers, and so on) is in the *Encyclopedia of Social Work,* mentioned above.

If you are curious about what kinds of positions are open to social workers with full professional education (M.A. or M.S.W. degree) of which some samples were given in Chapter Six, write to the National Association of Social Workers, 2 Park Avenue, New York, New York 10016, for an issue of *Personnel Information.* This is a listing of current openings for caseworkers, group workers, community workers, researchers, executives, all over the country. From it you'll get an idea of going salaries, work conditions, and so on.

Perhaps you'd like to talk directly to someone who is in social work and who knows it well. Two suggestions:

1. A request to the National Association of Social Workers (address above) will bring you the name and address of the president of the local chapter nearest to where you live. If the president can't arrange to see you, he'll see that someone else representing the chapter will.

2. If you are near a school of social work, a letter or phone call asking for an appointment to talk about your interest in a social work career will bring you an appointment with one of the faculty.

What you will find, wherever you turn, is that the profession of social work is keenly aware of the growing need for social workers, and through its national and local agencies it is involved in many recruitment efforts. Social workers and social agencies are glad to answer your inquiries and questions about social work. If you have the necessary qualifications to enter graduate education for social work or if you are still at the stage of trying to decide whether social work is or is not the career for you, you will find social workers ready and glad to help you by answering your questions or telling you what you want to know, either in person or by the many printed interpretations that are yours for the asking. If you qualify—social work wants you!

Index

About the Author

Mrs. Perlman says:

I fell into social work. When I graduated from college at the University of Minnesota I was bent on being a newspaper-woman (specialty "human-interest stories") or an advertising copywriter. But I needed money while I looked for these heady jobs, so I asked for and—to my amazement—got a job as a temporary caseworker in a family welfare agency. When at the summer's end the advertising job came along I was too deep in the poignant details of my clients' lives to be able to leave them.

Several years later, as I became increasingly intrigued and mystified by the complexities of human beings and their life cycles, I undertook graduate study in social work. I got my M.S. degree at the New York School of Social Work, Columbia University.

Family casework (particularly marital and parent-child problems), child guidance and school social work have been my fields of practice concentration. I have been able to combine my professional life with marriage and motherhood and travel and warm, good friendships—so it is partly on the basis of a happy personal experience that I commend social work to young people as a career.

For many years I have been on the faculty of the University of Chicago, where I am the Samuel Deutsch Professor of social work. While I've had a few short stories and poems published, most of my writing has been for professional journals. My book *Social Casework: A Problem-Solving Process* (1957) is used as a text in schools of social work and has been translated into seven foreign languages. My two most recent books are *Persona: Social Role and Personality* (1968), which deals with the stimuli for personal change in adults, and *Helping* (1969), which is an edited collection of articles by Charlotte Towle on social work and social casework.

72 9 8 7 6 5 4 3 2